Encountering
the
Presence

The Transforming Power of Truth

Encountering
the
Presence

The Transforming Power of Truth

Colin Urquhart

Destiny Image® Publishers, Inc.
P.O. Box 310
Shippensburg, PA 17257-0310

"Speaking to the Purposes of God for This Generation
and for the Generations to Come"

ISBN 0-7684-2018-0

For Worldwide Distribution
Printed in the U.S.A.

Second Edition: 1999

This book and all other Destiny Image, Revival Press,
and Treasure House books are available
at Christian bookstores and distributors worldwide.

For a U.S. bookstore nearest you, call **1-800-722-6774**.
For more information on foreign distributors, call **717-532-3040**.
Or reach us on the Internet: **http://www.reapernet.com**

Endorsements

"This book demonstrates how Colin Urquhart came to be one of the most respected Christian leaders in Britain and why he deserves to be heard and read."

—R.T. Kendall
Westminster Chapel, London

"I have known Colin for more than 25 years and have ministered with him on many occasions. I have watched him grow and develop in the powerful international ministry of faith and revival in the power of the Spirit that he has today. This book, *Encountering the Presence: The Transforming Power of Truth* is the very best of Colin Urquhart.

"One great chapter, 'Truth and Discipleship,' points us to what discipleship is. We have a wonderful story to tell about how Jesus came to save us and that He performed many amazing signs and wonders. What is more wonderful still is that He has given the same authority to us so that we can continue His ministry and mission to the world. We want to glorify God in our lives if we truly love Him. Jesus said that we do this by bearing much fruit. We have to encounter the glory of His

Presence, and He wants to see that glory reflected in us by the way we live and the fruit we bear.

"Colin's heart of passion for revival comes through in the last chapter and will help and challenge us all. And for those who need healing, this book will be very helpful in their search for their own personal healing. Best of all, we can all benefit by learning how to handle our circumstances by faith and truth and living free from their dictates. I wholeheartedly recommend the book and believe that you will be glad that you read it."

—Don Double
Evangelist

"For too long the popular inherited idea of God is that He is The Great Absent One. In this century God has worked to halve the epitaph that the world was writing. From the birth of Pentecostalism in 1906 to the renewal of the established churches decades later, God has been making Himself known as The Present One.

"Many of us have experienced God, yet are still hungry for more; not just in big meetings, but day in and day out. Colin Urquhart's book exhorts, challenges, and offers practical wisdom for us all to live each day in God's Presence. It is a book that will not only lead you into the Presence of God, but also cause you to seek more of His Presence and to be one in whom God is pleased to dwell."

—J John
Speaker and Writer

"*Encountering the Presence* will refocus our energies for Christ, prayer, and our own need of being broken and available to God's Spirit. Fresh scriptural insight reveals how far we can stray from what God regards as normal church life. This book will hopefully play a part in bringing us to God's dynamic norm for His people."

—Gerald Coates
Speaker, Author, Broadcaster

Contents

Chapter One

Meeting With the Divine Presence

The musicians had been playing for three hours, unable to stop. For one hour the preacher had stood behind the pulpit, unable to begin his sermon. All over the building the people were meeting with God—some on their faces as they bowed before His throne; others on their feet with hands lifted and faces shining; still others seemingly lost in the wonder of His love. The glory of God was upon His people.

For over five years this has been a common experience in the congregation where I serve as senior pastor. It is wonderful to encounter God's Presence in such ways.

In February 1998 we were privileged to host a European conference of those with apostolic ministries, convened by Dr. Peter Wagner and others. The evening meetings were open to the public and many from our congregation attended. On the evening he was scheduled to preach, Dr. Wagner had to wait for a long time before he could come to the platform as the Spirit of God once again moved upon His people, revealing the

Presence of Jesus in glorious worship. When he finally did speak, Dr. Wagner commented that in all his extensive travels he had never before encountered such a sense of the Presence of God in worship. It is his abiding memory of the conference.

We are certainly a blessed people. Not every service is like this, however, because the Lord has taught us that we encounter His Presence in many different ways. As His children, our purpose in coming together is to meet with Him. He longs to meet with us, but He doesn't always do it in the same way. The Lord likes variety.

For our part, we seek to be open to whatever the Lord wants to do on each occasion. Of course, His Presence is always there in our worship because our focus is on meeting with Him, on drawing near to His throne of grace, on entering the Holy of Holies, rather than on simply singing a number of songs to Jesus.

Encountering His Presence

We also want to encounter Jesus in His Word in the same way people did when He walked among them preaching the gospel of the Kingdom. We want to encounter His Presence when we pray, so that our prayer and intercession are truly filled with His life and power. We expect to encounter Him through the anointing of the Spirit as He ministers in love to His children, and in communion, as we express our unity with Him.

We also encounter His Presence in one another. We are not merely isolated islands seeking independent experiences of the Almighty; we are His Body, a people of love seeking to express our growing love for Him and for one another.

Yet the things that God is graciously doing among us would not amount to much if we only met with Him when we came together for services. People encountered Jesus in the temple and in the synagogues, but they also encountered His Presence on the streets where He healed them, in the fields where He preached to them, and in the homes He visited to eat with them and meet their needs.

So the Lord has been teaching us to meet with Him and to know His Presence in a variety of ways. Encountering Him in our services is important, but it is equally important to encounter His Presence in our daily circumstances. He has called us to take His Presence into the world to impact the lives of others with His truth.

What is the point of the anointing if we come together only to be anointed and to rejoice in that anointing? God anoints us for ministry. He gives His Holy Spirit as His living Presence within us so that we can use the anointing of His love and power to bless and serve others. Unless that anointing leads to fruitfulness, we will gradually lose the sense of His hand being on us, and the move of the His Spirit will fade into nothing more than a good memory to tell to our children.

It's All About Jesus

It is for this reason that I do not want to talk further about what God is doing among us. We are blessed, but we are reaching out to the Lord for more and are expecting much greater things in the future. Like the apostle Paul, each of us should...

> ...press on to take hold of that for which Christ Jesus took hold of me. Brothers, I do not consider myself yet to have taken hold of it. But one thing I do: Forgetting what is behind and straining toward what is ahead, I press on toward the goal to win the prize for which God has called me heavenward in Christ Jesus. All of us who are mature should take such a view of things... (Philippians 3:12-15).

Instead of concentrating on what God is doing among us, the focus in this book will be on Jesus, on the way He wants us to encounter His Presence in our daily experiences as well as in worship; how He wants the congregations to which you and I belong to be a people who encounter Him because they walk in the truth and in the power and presence of His Spirit.

You see, the Lord does not want His glory to be only on your services, but on *you*, on your life, revealed in your daily experiences and relationships. There needs to be a consistency in your Christian walk so that whether or not you are having wonderful experiences, you will still know that you are encountering His Presence daily.

When this is the case, you will understand the truth of His promise to be with you always (see Heb. 13:5). You will not have to keep repeating the text in an attempt to convince yourself that He is around, even though you have no sense of His Presence. You will know His Presence with you always.

What is more, you will not be dependent on the pastor's saying that because we are gathered in His name, Jesus is among us. You will *know* His Presence, no matter what is going on around you.

Jesus wants to revive His Church. He wants to see His children walking in the truth, rejoicing in Him, and revealing His glory to a sin-wearied world. We are to know and speak of His glory. David says that we are to "speak of the glorious splendor of Your majesty," and to "tell of the power of Your awesome works" (Ps. 145:5-6). "Your saints," he says, "will tell of the glory of Your kingdom and speak of Your might, so that all men may know of Your mighty acts and the glorious splendor of Your kingdom" (Ps. 145:10-12).

When do you intend to start doing this? It will be too late when you are in Heaven! How can you speak of the glory unless you know the glory? How can you speak of His mighty acts without experiencing the power of His Presence for yourself?

Come with me now and encounter His Presence. Meet with the Truth that will set you free to worship Him in every area of your life.

Chapter Two

Truth Wrapped in a Person

Anyone who loves Jesus wants to meet with Him, to encounter Him personally. It is wonderful to experience the Lord's Presence in personal, face-to-face encounters. Such occasions are extremely rare for most Christians. Nevertheless, we *can* encounter the Presence of Jesus every day of our lives, in personal and powerful ways that will be more than memorable experiences. Knowing Jesus as the Truth will release His power into our lives and enable lives of faith that overcome the inevitable difficulties and problems we face.

You see, Truth is a person: Jesus.

He certainly wants you to encounter His Presence in a number of ways. He wants you to meet with Him in His love. He wants you to know that He is with you always, in experience, not theory. He desires that you be familiar with His glory, so that it is a present reality in your life and not only a hope for the future.

Jesus has made all of this possible. It is why He came to earth, full of grace and truth. Because He *is* Truth, it is only by laying hold of Him as the Truth that we can truly know Him and experience His Presence every day in the ways that He intends.

Contrary to what many assume, truth and fact are *not* the same. It is very important to distinguish the fundamental difference between them; otherwise, there will be great confusion in our lives.

Truth is ultimate reality; it is eternal. Jesus is the Truth because He is the eternal Son of God. The eternal will continue forever while the merely physical and temporary will fade and disappear. Jesus said, "Heaven and earth will pass away, but My words will never pass away" (Mt. 24:35). Because He is the Truth, His words are truth; and those words of truth are the words of eternal life.

The world, on the other hand, lives on *facts*, not truth. Facts are temporal. They may be *real*, but they are not *truth*. For example, we are surrounded by the *fact* of the physical creation: the earth upon which we walk, the world of nature that fills the earth, the air that we breathe, and the laws of physics that govern the creation, such as the law of gravity. Although creation came into being through Jesus, the creation is not Jesus. Neither are the fresh air we breathe nor the law of gravity. All these are *facts*, but they are not *truth*. Only Jesus Himself is Truth.

Then there are the facts of our individual experiences: the things that are said to us, the things that happen to us, the events that take place in our lives. We think of these as the truth because we know that they have truly happened. Our experiences are very real to us. But no matter how real they are, they still are only facts, not truth. Truth is a Person, Jesus, and outside of Him there is no truth.

The world, however, tries to convince us that there is truth apart from Jesus. This deception is now so much a part of people's thinking and makeup that it has become very easy for even Christians to be led astray. In reality, the world has no truth because it has rejected the One who *is* Truth:

The true light that gives light to every man was coming into the world. He was in the world, and though the world was made through Him, the world did not recognize Him. He came to that which was His own, but His own did not receive Him (John 1:9-11).

THE TRUTH

Down through the ages the central activity of the human race has been the search for truth. That quest has motivated philosophers, inspired religious leaders, and fired the imaginations of millions. Ever since the first humans traded the truth for a lie in the Garden of Eden, mankind has struggled to get it back. Is there absolute truth? If so, where is it to be found? Many who claimed to have found it have, in the end, only deceived themselves and any who followed them. The question of truth is more than simply a philosophical musing; it gets right at the very root of the meaning of life itself.

Pontius Pilate was confronted with this question in a very literal way. Jesus, having suffered the humiliation of a mock trial at the home of the high priest, was brought before the Roman governor by the Jewish religious leaders. Pilate, who had heard rumors about this man, asked Jesus, "Are You the king of the Jews?" (Jn. 18:33) Jesus answered:

... "My kingdom is not of this world. If it were, My servants would fight to prevent My arrest by the Jews. But now My kingdom is from another place." ... "You are right in saying I am a king. In fact, for this reason I was born, and for this I came into the world, to testify to the truth. Everyone on the side of truth listens to Me" (John 18:36-37).

Pilate's response was simply, *"What is truth?"* (Jn. 18:38) Poor Pilate! The Truth was right before his very eyes, but he was too blind to see it!

Jesus Christ is Truth. He Himself stated this plainly enough when He told His disciples, *"I am* the way and the *truth* and the life. No one comes to the Father except through Me" (Jn. 14:6). The full force of that proclamation in the Greek is lost somewhat in English translation. In Greek the word for "I am" is *eimi,* while *ego* is the first person pronoun "I." If you wish to say "I am," you use *eimi;* to simply say "I," you use *ego.* The use of either word alone is sufficient for most meanings. When both *eimi* and *ego* are used together, however, it indicates a point of tremendous emphasis. Such is the case here. Jesus stressed His identity as the Truth by twice stating "I": "I, I am," or "I, even I, am." When Moses asked for His name, God told him it was "I AM WHO I AM" (see Ex. 3:13-14). Jesus' statement in John 14:6 is similar. When He says "I, even I," He is affirming that He is God. So the emphasis in this verse is not on the way, truth, and life as much as it is on the One who personifies them. In other words, this statement concentrates on the *person* of Jesus: *I, even I, am the way, I, even I, am the truth, I, even I, am the life.*

Normally, we don't think of truth in such personal terms. Much of the world regards truth as an abstract, an ideal, a concept that is relative to one's circumstances and may even change depending on the situation. Such a view is the complete opposite of that which is given in the Word of God. The Gospel of John opens with a profound statement regarding Truth: "In the beginning was the *Word,* and the *Word* was with God, and the *Word* was God. He was with God in the beginning" (Jn. 1:1-2). Jesus is the *Word* who was with God and who was God. "Word" in the Greek is *logos,* and refers here to the expression of the very essence, being, and nature of God. The same word is used in chapter 17 when Jesus prays to His

Father regarding His disciples: "Sanctify them by the truth; Your *word* is truth" (Jn. 17:17). Jesus, the *Word*—the eternal *logos* of God—*is* the Truth.

*If Jesus is the Truth, then there is **no** truth outside of Jesus.* This is why He says, "No one comes to the Father except through Me." There is only *one way* to the Father: Jesus. There is only *one truth* for the world: Jesus. There is only *one life* that is full and everlasting: Jesus.

Truth vs. Facts

The world knows a lot of facts and is deceived in the belief that these constitute truth. Facts are merely facts. They are not truth. Truth is a Person, Jesus, and He is eternal. Facts may be real, but they are not eternal. Facts simply tell us about the circumstances of our lives *right now.*

Here is an example. A man may be told that he has cancer. Although that may be a fact—the cancer may be *real*—it is not the *truth*. The truth is what the Bible says about Jesus and sickness:

> *But He was wounded for our transgressions, He was bruised for our iniquities: the chastisement of our peace was upon Him; and **with His stripes we are healed*** (Isaiah 53:5 KJV),

and

> *Who His own self bare our sins in His own body on the tree, that we, being dead to sins, should live unto righteousness: **by whose stripes ye were healed*** (1 Peter 2:24 KJV).

So it is a fact that the man has cancer, but the truth is that by the stripes of Jesus he is healed. What matters, then, is whether the man believes the *facts* or the *truth*. The same principle can be applied to other areas of experience. You can have a need; that is a fact. Yet the truth is that in Christ you have all things, and every promise of His provision (see Rom. 8:32; Phil. 4:19). You choose whether to believe the facts or the truth.

Facts can never alter truth because truth is eternal and unchanging, but *truth can change the facts*. It is really quite simple; it depends on which we believe. Whenever we pray, we must pray according to the Word—according to the Truth—not according to the facts. The way some people pray makes it clear that they believe the facts rather than believing the truth to *change* the facts. This doesn't mean we *deny* the facts. That's totally unrealistic. We can't deny the realities of the cancer or the empty bank account, but we need to see them for what they really are: facts and nothing more. The truth is much greater than the facts because Jesus Himself is the Truth. Whenever we come to Jesus in prayer, or for ministry, or in any other way, we need to be constantly aware that we are laying hold of the Truth.

No matter what reality we know in the natural realm, there is a greater reality in the supernatural realm. The supernatural can invade the natural and change the facts and circumstances with which we are so familiar. Taking an obvious example, as believers we can choose to sin, seeking to please ourselves rather than God. We are guilty; the sin in our lives is a fact. But there is a truth that is able to change the fact. Through the forgiveness of Jesus Christ, our sin is eradicated; it is so completely forgiven that it is as though we had never sinned. God will never hold that sin against us or mention it at all on the day of judgment. It isn't a matter of denying the fact of our sin, but of recognizing that there is a truth that is higher and greater than the facts. When that truth is brought to bear upon the facts, the facts are changed.

It is the same with sickness. Sickness is a fact. If you are sick, there is no point in denying it. Jesus is not sickness, however, so sickness is not the truth. We have already seen from the Word of God that Jesus, the Truth, bore our infirmities, carried our sicknesses, and healed us by His stripes. That is the eternal, supernatural Truth that is greater than the temporal, natural fact of sickness. When we bring the eternal Truth to bear upon the facts, the facts can be changed. Through the power of what Jesus Christ has accomplished for us, we can receive our healing. As we do so, we experience the reality, the Presence of His love, mercy, and grace; *the Truth sets us free*!

Other physical realities can also be completely negated by the Truth. For example, when Jesus ascended into Heaven He contradicted the law of gravity because the law of gravity is only a fact and Jesus is the Truth who can transcend the fact. When He took Peter, James, and John with Him onto the Mount of Transfiguration, the three disciples saw His physical, earthly body transformed into His glorious body. The fact of His human body was overshadowed by the truth that He was the glorified Son of God. His true nature was revealed to those disciples as a foretaste of the glory to come.

Full of Grace and Truth

Jesus has always been the Word of God. He is the Truth by whom and through whom all things were created. Remember the words of John:

In the beginning was the Word, and the Word was with God, and the Word was God. He was with God in the beginning. Through Him all things were made; without Him nothing was made that has been made. ... The Word became flesh and made His dwelling among us. We have seen His glory, the glory of the One and Only, who came from the Father, full of grace and truth. ... From the fullness of His grace we have all received one blessing after another. For the law was given through

Moses; grace and truth came through Jesus Christ
(John 1:1-3,14,16-17).

When God created, all He had to do was speak, and the
universe was born. Worlds were formed and the stars were set
in their courses. The earth brought forth life by His command.
Then there came the time when that Word through whom creation had come into being took on human flesh and lived
among mankind on earth. John said that when Jesus came as
the Word of God made flesh, He was "full of grace and truth"
(1:14). Grace is usually described as the free unmerited favor
of God. Stated very simply, that means that *God wants to give
everything to those who deserve **nothing***. In fact, grace is so
amazing that it means receiving from God the very *opposite* of
what we deserve. Qualifying for grace is easy: Simply admit
that you deserve nothing. I qualify very easily.

Jesus, the Good Shepherd, said, "I have come that they
[His sheep] may have life, and have it to the full" (Jn. 10:10b).
On another occasion He assured His disciples, "Do not be
afraid, little flock, for your Father has been pleased to give you
the kingdom" (Lk. 12:32). The Son of God became the Son of
man in order to give us what we don't deserve. The very Word
of God, the Word of Truth, became the ultimate expression of
the magnitude of God's amazing grace in giving us the fullness of His life. He put the Kingdom of Heaven to live and
grow within us in order that we might live the life of the Kingdom here on earth and enjoy the full inheritance of it eternally in Heaven.

Since Jesus is full of grace and truth, there is nothing in
Him that is contrary to either grace or truth; nothing in Him is
a denial of God's desire to give. God wants to give freely to all,
but there are two particular conditions for receiving from Him.
Jesus explained what is required when He said, "The time has

come....The kingdom of God is near. *Repent and believe* the good news!" (Mk. 1:15)

Repent and believe. Repentance is turning around to God; having a change of mind and bringing our thinking in line with God's thinking. Or, in other words, *repentance is bringing our thinking in line with the truth.* There is no good news until we face the bad news that our sin separates us from God and puts us in a place of condemnation, under the judgment that we deserve. The good news is that Jesus, the Truth, came to us bringing the words of life and of God's Kingdom. He sacrificed His life for us on the cross that we might be forgiven of everything in our lives that contradicts the truth. Through Him we have received God's grace, which imparts to us the gift of eternal life, the life in all its fullness that Jesus came to give.

John recorded a wonderful truth from Jesus in his Gospel:

I tell you the truth, whoever hears My word and believes Him who sent Me has eternal life and will not be condemned; he has crossed over from death to life (John 5:24).

*According to Jesus, those who hear and believe Him have eternal life **right now** as a **present reality**! They have **already** crossed over from death into life!* This verse also shows us that turning around to God's truth in *repentance* must be accompanied by faith—*believing* the truth. A person is born again only when he *believes* the truth of what God has done in Jesus Christ. This is what Paul meant when he wrote to the Ephesians:

And you also were included in Christ when you heard the word of truth, the gospel of your salvation. Having believed, you were marked in Him with a seal, the promised Holy Spirit, who is a deposit guaranteeing our inheritance until the redemption of those who are God's possession—to the praise of His glory (Ephesians 1:13-14).

There is a sequence of events here. *Hearing* the gospel, the word of truth, we *believed*; and having believed, we were *marked* with the seal of the Holy Spirit as a guarantee to us that we belong to God and will inherit His Kingdom. *Hearing alone is not enough; we must believe what we have heard.* Whether that hearing came through reading the Scripture, through hearing a sermon, through the testimony of another believer, or through reading some Christian literature, somehow we each heard the word of truth, the gospel of salvation, the good news of what God did for us in Jesus Christ. Through His grace working in our hearts we believed, and upon believing we were sealed in Him with the promised Holy Spirit. At that moment we were born again of the Spirit of God. At that moment we were brought out of the dominion of darkness and into the shadowless light of the Kingdom of God. At that moment we were delivered out of the bondage of satan and into the glorious liberty of the sons of God. At that moment our old lives died and we were made new creations in Christ. At that moment everything changed, and it will take us the rest of our lives to understand all that He did for us.

This whole wonderful sequence of events began with *hearing* the truth. That's why it was so important for Jesus to become a man and dwell among us to give us the revelation of truth, and why it was necessary for Him to give His life on the cross. *His death delivered us from everything that contradicts the truth and freed us from all the lies and deceptions of the enemy.*

James tells us that God "chose to give us birth through the word of truth" (Jas. 1:18a). Without that revelation of truth it would be impossible to understand God, His plan and purpose for our lives, or what He wants to accomplish in us. We would not be able to explain why He wanted to live in us in the Holy Spirit or what He wanted to make of us as His children. Through His grace, however, He has revealed the truth to us.

Now we can rejoice that we have received the life of His Kingdom and that His Spirit dwells within us, enabling us to live according to the truth.

THE GOSPEL OF TRUTH

Jesus came bearing the gospel of truth. Everything He said and did was truth. By word and example He taught how we are to live as children of the Kingdom here on earth in preparation for our lives in eternity with Him in glory. Scripture presents the Kingdom of God as a progression: It has come, it is coming now, and it will come in its fullness at the return of Christ.

Likewise, the New Testament pictures salvation as a three-stage process with past, present, and future aspects:

1. *Justification.* Because we have put our faith in Jesus, the Truth, we *have been saved* immediately, completely, and eternally from the *penalty of sin.*

2. *Sanctification.* As we grow in Christ daily and continually, we *are being saved* from the *power of sin*, the powers of darkness, and all other things that come against us.

3. *Glorification.* The Scriptures assure us that one future day we *will be saved* from the *presence of sin.* Delivered from the judgment that we deserve, we will then enter into the full inheritance that is ours in Christ Jesus.

Because we are heirs to God's Kingdom, it is important for us to learn to receive everything that Jesus wants to impart to us as children of God. Just as we became disciples only by believing the truth, it is only by believing the truth that we can *live* as disciples and receive all that He wants to give us. We have already seen that the truth is greater than facts and that it can overcome and change the facts in our lives. The four Gospels tell how great crowds of people came and flocked around Jesus. He was a marvelous teacher, but it was more than just His teaching that drew them. The great and powerful events that took place in His ministry were a strong attraction. *Crowds gathered not just to hear the truth, but to have an encounter with the Truth.* They came with many different needs, but also with a faith and expectation that Jesus, the Truth, could impact their lives in such a way that the facts and circumstances of their lives would be changed.

Matthew gives us an excellent example of Jesus' teaching. Chapters 5, 6, and 7 of his Gospel comprise what is commonly known as the Sermon on the Mount. Whether this was a sermon that Jesus taught on one particular occasion, or whether it is a collection of His sayings that have been brought together into a typical sermon is of little importance. Everything here recorded from the mouth of Jesus is the truth. The overall theme is living the life of the Kingdom. It would be totally impossible for a nonbeliever to live the life that is described in these chapters. However, anyone who has come to faith in Jesus Christ and has the Holy Spirit living in him has been empowered to live the lifestyle that Jesus defines here.

Jesus is the Truth and He came speaking the gospel of truth. He taught with authority because His word was truth. Consider these examples:

- "**You have heard** that it was said…'Do not murder….' **But I tell you** that anyone who is angry with his brother will be subject to judgment" (Mt. 5:21-22a).

- "**You have heard** that it was said, 'Do not commit adultery.' **But I tell you** that anyone who looks at a woman lustfully has already committed adultery with her in his heart" (Mt. 5:27-28).

- "**You have heard** that it was said, 'Eye for eye, and tooth for tooth.' **But I tell you**, Do not resist an evil person. If someone strikes you on the right cheek, turn to him the other also" (Mt. 5:38-39).

- "**You have heard** that it was said, 'Love your neighbor and hate your enemy.' **But I tell you**: Love your enemies and pray for those who persecute you, that you may be sons of your Father in heaven" (Mt. 5:43-45a).

- "When Jesus had finished saying these things, the crowds were amazed at His teaching, because **He taught as one who had authority**, and not as their teachers of the law" (Mt. 7:28-29).

This is truth as Jesus proclaimed it. The people were accustomed to teachers who legitimized their authority by referring to great teachers of an earlier day. Jesus was different. He taught on His own authority, an authority given to Him by His Father. Jesus spoke truth, which does not change according to culture, language, public opinion, or anything else.

It is truth for every man, woman, and child walking on this earth. The chapters of Matthew's Gospel that follow the Sermon on the Mount record instance after instance of personal encounters with Jesus; people encountering the Presence of God in their midst, encountering the Truth. Every encounter with the Truth changed the facts of their lives. These encounters will be examined more closely in the next chapter. If we believe the Truth, we too will encounter His Presence and will see the promises of God fulfilled in our lives.

So Truth is a Person, Jesus Christ, who is much greater than all He has made, greater than all our circumstances. If we believe the Truth, any of the facts of our lives, any experience, any problem, any dilemma or need that arises, can be changed by the Truth that is greater than all. We can encounter His Presence daily!

Chapter Three

The Truth That Changes the Facts

Have you ever asked about someone's welfare and heard the reply, "Oh, I'm doing all right, under the circumstances"? Perhaps you have even used that line yourself. Whether it is too little money, poor health, unemployment, or whatever, the statement implies an attempt to make the best of a negative situation. Most people, including many Christians, define the quality of their lives by the nature of their personal circumstances. This is deceptive because, as we have already seen, circumstances reflect facts, *not* truth. *Jesus is the Truth who can overcome the circumstances.*

God doesn't want us to be "under the circumstances," but to rise above them by believing and speaking the truth over our lives and our situations. Then the truth can change our circumstances and bring them into line with God's perfect will and purpose. The apostle Paul wrote to the Galatians, "It is for freedom that Christ has set us free. Stand firm, then, and do not let yourselves be burdened again by a yoke of slavery"

(Gal. 5:1). Although Paul's words were in the specific context of religious legalism, they apply equally to every area of our lives as believers. It is not God's purpose that we be slaves to *any* earthly reality, including our day-to-day circumstances. Through Christ we have the victory (see 1 Cor. 15:57). He wants us to live as *victors*, not *victims*; to *reign* over life rather than be *ruled* by it. Paul expressed it this way to the Romans:

For if, by the trespass of the one man, death reigned through that one man, how much more will those who receive God's abundant provision of grace and of the gift of righteousness reign in life through the one man, Jesus Christ (Romans 5:17).

Negative circumstances in our lives originate from either one of two main sources. The first is those situations that arise through no fault of our own and are simply an inevitable part of life in a fallen world. The second source is our own human weaknesses: selfishness, poor judgment, pride, disobedience, personal sin, and so on. In either case God's power to change the circumstances is the same; the nature and degree of *our* response depend on the situation. For example, if our own sin has put us in a difficult spot, our proper response is to confess the sin, claim God's forgiveness in the name of Jesus, and believe and speak the truth over our lives in that situation. On the other hand, when trouble comes of its own accord, we need to lay hold of the truth of God's desire and power to release us, and believe and claim that truth in order to experience victory. Either way, *freedom comes from encountering and believing the truth.*

If you have placed your faith in the truth of the gospel, you have been born again and are in relationship with Jesus Christ. He wants you to learn to walk by faith, not by sight, and to trust that day by day the truth will overcome the facts of the adverse circumstances of your life. Faith in the truth enables you to encounter the Presence of Jesus in those circumstances.

Jesus came to do more than simply model a moral life; He came to atone for our sins by His death on the cross and to guarantee eternal life for us by His resurrection. His purpose also was to enable us to walk in righteousness and enjoy all the rights and privileges that are ours as citizens of the Kingdom of God.

Everything that Jesus said and did served to fulfill these purposes. We have already seen how those who followed Jesus encountered the truth in His words when they listened to His teaching, such as in the Sermon on the Mount. Matthew follows his account of the sermon with a series of personal encounters with Jesus in which individuals came face-to-face with the Truth and were forever changed. Each of these encounters is significant in revealing different aspects of how the truth overcomes circumstances: disease, nature, and the demonic spirit realm.

Truth Overcomes Disease

Surely there is no occasion when we long to encounter the Presence of Jesus more than in sickness. Matthew records a series of healings by Jesus that illustrates His character and attitude toward physical disease and those afflicted by it. As soon as Jesus came down from the mountain He was met by a leper. Consider Matthew's account:

A man with leprosy came and knelt before Him and said, "Lord, if You are willing, You can make me clean." Jesus reached out His hand and touched the man. "I am willing," He said. "Be clean!" Immediately he was cured of his leprosy (Matthew 8:2-3).

Jesus' Willingness to Heal

There is much of significance in this brief account. The leper approached Jesus with "conditional faith"; he expressed no doubt of Jesus' *ability* to heal, only of His *willingness* to do so. He was so accustomed to being shunned because of his disease that he half expected Jesus to react the same way. Jesus simply removed the condition. He *touched* the man and said, "I am willing. Be clean."

This is important. It was not necessary for Jesus to *touch* the leper to heal him. Jesus' touch was an act of great compassion. Because of the repulsive nature of his disease, this leper had probably had no physical contact with any other people, except possibly for other lepers, in years. By the *action* of His touch and the words of His mouth, Jesus demonstrated His *willingness* to heal. Jesus is the same yesterday, today, and forever (see Heb. 13:8). *He **wants** to heal.* Sickness is only a fact. The leprosy was only a fact, not the truth. *The leper encountered the Truth, Jesus, and that encounter changed the fact of his leprosy.* He was cleansed immediately. The truth overcame his circumstances.

Jesus' Authority to Heal

Jesus not only has the *willingness* to heal; He also has the *authority* to do so. Look at the next several verses in Matthew's account:

> *When Jesus had entered Capernaum, a centurion came to Him, asking for help. "Lord," he said, "my servant lies at home paralyzed and in terrible suffering." Jesus said to him, "I will go and heal him." The centurion replied, "Lord, I do not deserve to have You come under my roof. But just say the word, and my servant will be healed. For I myself am a man under authority, with soldiers under me. I tell this one, 'Go,' and he goes; and that one, 'Come,' and he comes. I say to my servant, 'Do*

this,' and he does it." When Jesus heard this, He was astonished and said to those following Him, "I tell you the truth, I have not found anyone in Israel with such great faith." ... Then Jesus said to the centurion, "Go! It will be done just as you believed it would." And his servant was healed at that very hour (Matthew 8:5-10,13).

Jesus was amazed by the great faith of this man who was not even a Jew, but a Roman soldier. The centurion recognized that all Jesus had to do was speak the word of healing and it would be done. The truth *spoken* would overcome the fact of illness. There is such *authority* in the truth.

The centurion understood authority. His authority over the soldiers under him derived from his submission to the authority of the officers over him. He could exercise his authority only as long as he remained submitted to the authority of his superiors. If he was insubordinate and overstepped his bounds, he would lose his authority and be removed from his position. The centurion's authority depended upon his obedience to his superiors. In the same way, the centurion recognized that Jesus exercised power and authority because He submitted Himself to the authority of God. Therefore, it was necessary only for Jesus to speak with authority over illness, and the centurion's servant would be healed.

Throughout His life on earth, Jesus lived in complete, conscious, and willing submission to His Father. This was the secret of His authority and the source of His power to perform great works. Of all the Gospel writers, John probably provides us with the fullest picture of the relationship that existed between God the Father and Christ the Son. John makes it clear that Jesus did not come to do His own will, but the will of His Father who sent Him. Consider these statements Jesus made:

- "My food...is to do the will of Him who sent Me and to finish His work" (Jn. 4:34).

- "...I tell you the truth, the Son can do nothing by Himself; He can do only what He sees His Father doing, because whatever the Father does the Son also does" (Jn. 5:19).

- "For I have come down from heaven not to do My will but to do the will of Him who sent Me" (Jn. 6:38).

- ..."When you have lifted up the Son of Man, then you will know that I am the one I claim to be and that I do nothing on My own but speak just what the Father has taught Me" (Jn. 8:28).

- "For I did not speak of My own accord, but the Father who sent Me commanded Me what to say and how to say it. I know that His command leads to eternal life. So whatever I say is just what the Father has told Me to say" (Jn. 12:49-50).

- "Don't you believe that I am in the Father, and that the Father is in Me? The words I say to you are not just My own. Rather, it is the Father, living in Me, who is doing His work" (Jn. 14:10).

Whenever we hear Jesus speaking, we hear the Father speaking. Whenever we see Jesus working, we see the Father working. Jesus never worked independently of His Father, which is why He could say, "I and the Father are one" (Jn. 10:30); "Anyone who has seen Me has seen the Father" (Jn. 14:9b); and "The Father is greater than I" (Jn. 14:28c). Jesus submitted to the will of His Father even to the point of dying on the cross, which is why He prayed in the Garden of Gethsemane, "Father...not My will, but Yours be done" (Lk. 22:42). Jesus was so submitted to the authority of His Father that He could speak with authority, and *whenever He spoke with authority, the truth changed the facts.*

Jesus told the centurion, "Go! It will be done just as you believed it would." The centurion's servant was healed at that very hour. That is still God's word today: *It will be done just as you believed.* Truth gives us authority. That authority is greater than the facts because it is a supernatural authority that comes from God Himself. It will be manifested in our lives as long as we are submitted to God's authority. That means that not only do we *call* Him Lord but we also allow Him to *be* Lord in our lives.

Jesus' Compassion to Heal

In the next several verses from chapter 8 of Matthew we see another quality of Jesus as the truth overcoming disease: His compassion. Matthew writes:

When Jesus came into Peter's house, He saw Peter's mother-in-law lying in bed with a fever. He touched her hand and the fever left her, and she got up and began to wait on Him. When evening came, many who were demon-possessed were brought to Him, and He drove out the spirits with a word and healed all the sick. This was to fulfill what was spoken through the prophet Isaiah: "He took up our infirmities and carried our diseases" (Matthew 8:14-17).

The simple, matter-of-fact way Matthew describes these encounters gives them a warm, genuine human quality. Apparently, Jesus had entered Peter's home for the night and found Peter's mother-in-law sick from a fever. A simple, gentle touch from the Master changed the situation completely. The fever left, and she rose and began to serve Him. The account gives no indication that Jesus said anything. He simply touched her and the fever left.

When the power of God touches us, we may not hear any audible words, but we are left with no doubt that His Truth has changed us in some dynamic way. *His Presence has invaded the natural circumstances of our lives and transformed them.* God doesn't do these things as ends in themselves. Rather, He wants to meet with us, provide for us, set us free, heal us—whatever is necessary—so that, like Peter's mother-in-law, we can rise up and serve Him.

It was the end of a long day. Jesus had been teaching and ministering and undoubtedly was tired and probably hungry. He needed rest. Yet, in the evening, when things normally should slow down, people with needs were still coming to Jesus. He cast demons out of those who were possessed, and healed all the sick who came to Him. How many people are we talking about here? Matthew doesn't say. Jesus may have been up well into the night. He didn't turn any away, no matter what His *own* needs were. He didn't reach a certain point and say, "Please, no more tonight. Come back tomorrow." Jesus did not turn away those in need who came to Him.

No matter who they were or what their need was, whether demonic deliverance or physical healing, everyone who came that night experienced the deep compassion of Jesus and encountered the Truth that set them free. Possession by demonic powers is not the ultimate Truth. It is only a fact. Physical sickness is not the ultimate Truth. It is only a fact. The ultimate Truth is Jesus, and the supernatural power flowing through Him overcomes the circumstances of disease.

Matthew explains in verse 17 that these things happened to fulfill what was spoken through the prophet Isaiah: "He took up our infirmities and carried our diseases." The quote is from Isaiah 53:4, one verse from a remarkable chapter describing the meaning and significance of the crucifixion and the atoning death of Jesus. Since the cross had not yet come at this point in Jesus' ministry, why does Matthew refer to it here? During His earthly ministry, Jesus was limited in His healing work to those people whom He met or who came to Him. Through His death on the cross He accomplished and made available to all people of every generation the salvation, healing, and deliverance that were available only to a limited number of one generation in one tiny area of the world during His earthly ministry. The cross was that once-for-eternity event that made possible the release of God's life, power, and victory in the lives of any and all who believe in Jesus Christ and claim Him as Savior and Lord.

Jesus has already accomplished everything needed for our salvation, healing, and deliverance. He did it on the cross. There is no reason for us to ask the Lord to do what He has already done. He wants us to believe that He *has* done it so that *our faith in what He has **already** accomplished will bring the truth to bear upon the circumstances of our lives and change those circumstances.* Jesus made the sacrifice for our sins on the cross. When we sin as Christians, that doesn't mean Jesus has to die again for our forgiveness. He died once and for all, forever. We confess our sins, claiming forgiveness based on what Jesus has already done. By the same token, if we are sick, Jesus doesn't have to do anything new in order to heal us. He has already done it. Just as faith lays hold of His forgiving grace, so faith lays hold of His healing grace.

Truth Overcomes Nature

Throughout His life on earth, Jesus, the Truth, came against all manner of human "reality" and transformed it, demonstrating clearly by word and deed that the physical realm in which we live is temporary and changing, while the spiritual realm is eternal. Physical disease, inescapably "real" by human standards, was to Jesus merely a temporary fact that could be completely changed by a word or a touch.

This power of the truth to change circumstances extends also to the natural realm. If there is any reality less subject to man's control than disease, it is the forces of nature. Matthew describes how Jesus' disciples encountered the Truth in a totally unexpected way:

> *Then He got into the boat and His disciples followed Him. Without warning, a furious storm came up on the lake, so that the waves swept over the boat. But Jesus was sleeping. The disciples went and woke Him, saying, "Lord, save us! We're going to drown!" He replied, "You of little faith, why are you so afraid?" Then He got up and rebuked the winds and the waves, and it was completely calm. The men were amazed and asked, "What kind of man is this? Even the winds and the waves obey Him!"* (Matthew 8:23-27)

After His busy evening of healing ministry, Jesus was tired and fell asleep in the boat in which He and His disciples were crossing the Sea of Galilee. He didn't wake up even when the storm arose and tossed the boat to and fro. While the disciples quaked in terror, Jesus slept on. What was the difference? The disciples were focused on the storm—a mere fact—while Jesus knew the truth that could overcome the fact. The disciples forgot that in the presence of the Truth, Jesus, they were perfectly safe. That is why Jesus rebuked them for their lack of faith when they woke Him out of fear. The *reality* of their situation was a dangerous, frightening storm. The *truth* of their situation was that they were in the company of He who had authority over the storm. Jesus opened their eyes to that truth by ending the storm with the words, "Quiet! Be still!" (see Mk. 4:39) Immediately it was "completely calm."

When the truth came against the fact of the storm, the fact had to give way to the truth. The truth is much greater even than the elements. Jesus believed that when He spoke the storm would cease. Faith is being sure and certain. It isn't saying something and hoping for the best. Jesus was utterly convinced that the word of truth spoken with authority would change the circumstances in which He was placed. *Likewise, the Lord wants us to demonstrate that same quality of faith so that we will believe the truth and speak it over the circumstances of our lives.*

The disciples were afraid because they were focused on the facts. Believing the *facts* results in *fear*; believing the *truth* results in *faith*. Jesus rebuked the disciples for their unbelief, not only because they didn't really understand that they were safe with Him but also because none of *them* stood up and rebuked the wind! They must have perceived that this was something coming against them. Sometimes God wants us to stand up to those things that come against us. He wants us, in faith, to speak to that mountain and move it in the power of the truth. The storms of life are nothing more than mountains that need to be moved, and we are given the authority to see them moved. Jesus dwells in the hearts of all who have trusted Him as Lord and Savior. He is in us! The apostle Paul wrote of the "mystery, which is Christ in you, the hope of glory" (Col. 1:27b). *We have Jesus, the very Word of God, the Truth, living in us.* When we stand in that reality we can wield the "sword of the Spirit, which is the word of God" (Eph. 6:17b), by speaking the word of truth over our circumstances, and see for ourselves that truth changes the facts.

Truth Overcomes the Demonic Spirit Realm

While the disciples were still trying to adjust their thinking to the reality of Jesus' authority over nature, they witnessed a powerful example of His authority over the spirit realm.

When He arrived at the other side in the region of the Gadarenes, two demon-possessed men coming from the tombs met Him. They were so violent that no one could pass that way. "What do You want with us, Son of God?" they shouted. "Have You come here to torture us

before the appointed time?" Some distance from them a
large herd of pigs was feeding. The demons begged
Jesus, "If You drive us out, send us into the herd of
pigs." He said to them, "Go!" So they came out and
went into the pigs, and the whole herd rushed down the
steep bank into the lake and died in the water (Matthew
8:28-32).

Notice that the demons possessing the two men knew
immediately who Jesus was. They addressed Him as the Son
of God. Notice too their demeanor with Him. Matthew says
that the two men were so violent that no one could pass that
way. They were dangerous. Yet when Jesus appeared, they didn't
rush down in violent, aggressive attack, but approached in
pleading and fear. They recognized the power and authority of
the Truth confronting them.

Jesus does not even attempt to have a conversation with the
demons. He simply issues the single command, "Go!" and the
demonic spirits have no choice but to leave. Their power and
destructive nature are revealed as they enter the herd of pigs
and cause the entire herd to rush into the lake and drown. No
matter how powerful demonic forces appear to be, it is clear
that the power of the truth is greater.

God wants us to know that because we have the Truth living in us, we do not have to put up with any oppression or any
attack from the enemy. It is never true to say that the devil has
us in a vice or in bondage, because He that is in us—the Spirit of Truth—is greater than he that is in the world (see 1 Jn.
4:4). There is power in the truth. The truth lives in us if we
have the Spirit and the Word of God in us. It doesn't matter
whose mouth speaks the truth because the power is in the
truth, not the mouth. So the truth in our mouths is just as powerful as the truth in Jesus' mouth. *The Spirit of Truth living in*
us enables us to speak the truth in faith with authority so that

the power of God can be released into our circumstances. Whenever the enemy attacks, we can take the shield of faith and the sword of the Spirit and see the devil run as we submit ourselves to God (see Jas. 4:7).

When we submit ourselves to God, we submit ourselves to the Truth and to thinking and believing as He does about the particular circumstances in which we find ourselves. This needs to be a continual, daily, moment-by-moment submission. We can never rest from believing, living, and walking in the truth because the enemy never rests in his efforts to deceive and discourage us. We have within us all the resources necessary to rise up against everything that comes against us and to overcome in Jesus' name.

God rejoices to see His children overcoming and walking by faith in the victory that He has given us through the Lord Jesus Christ. We are not victims; we are victors! Let's live accordingly! If only we Christians would recognize and believe the power and authority that we have, we would not cave in so easily to the difficulties that arise. Neither would we go around seeking counseling as much as we do, nor dwell so much on our problems. Instead, we would rise up in faith and overcome those things that come against us. Jesus is the Truth that overcomes the circumstances of our lives.

You have His Presence within you. Therefore you can speak His word with His authority and release the power of His Truth and of His Presence into every situation, if you choose to do so.

Chapter Four

Portal to the Eternal Presence

How do we bring to bear on our lives the truth that overcomes and changes our circumstances? Through faith. The truth is of little benefit to us if we do not believe it. Furthermore, that belief must be more than simple mental acknowledgment. Effective faith is applied faith—faith put into *action*, not simply talked about. Faith is not so much something we *have* as something we *do*. We exhibit faith through our *actions* even more than through our words. This is what James meant when he wrote:

> *What good is it, my brothers, if a man claims to have faith but has no deeds? Can such faith save him? ... In the same way, faith by itself, if it is not accompanied by action, is dead. But someone will say, "You have faith; I have deeds." Show me your faith without deeds, and I will show you my faith by what I do* (James 2:14,17-18).

Genuine faith gives rise to works of faith. Must faith then always be present in order for God to work? Generally, the answer is yes, although in His sovereign majesty God sometimes chooses to act even in situations where there seems to be little faith. Often, the evidence of the working of God is in proportion to the amount of faith present. One thing is certain: Where there *is* faith God *always* works because that is what He has promised to do. He always responds to genuine faith and is willing to meet us where we are, whether our faith is great or small. Mark tells the story of a man who brought his demon-possessed son to the disciples, who were unable to deliver the boy. Appealing to Jesus, who had just returned with Peter, James, and John from the Mount of Transfiguration, the distraught father pleaded:

> *"...If You can do anything, take pity on us and help us."*
> *" 'If You can'?" said Jesus. "Everything is possible for him who believes." Immediately the boy's father exclaimed, "I do believe; help me overcome my unbelief!"* (Mark 9:22-24)

Jesus responded to the man's faith and cast the demon out of his son.

On the other hand, lack of faith can hinder the work of God. Once, when Jesus visited His hometown of Nazareth, "He could not do any miracles there, except lay His hands on a few sick people and heal them. And He was amazed at their lack of faith" (Mk. 6:5-6a). What was the nature of their unbelief? Simply put, they did not believe Jesus to be the Truth. Nazareth was a tiny village. Growing up there, Jesus would have been well known by everyone in town. It was difficult for them to accept the idea that the carpenter's son they had known for years was in truth the Messiah sent by God to be the Savior of the world. Consequently, they missed out on experiencing the power and blessings of the Presence of God in their midst. Such is the power of unbelief.

Clearly, then, faith is critical in responding to the truth. The power of faith in the truth means that nothing is impossible.

Jesus not only said that "with God all things are possible" (Mt. 19:26) but also that "everything is possible for him who believes" (Mk. 9:23). *When we believe the truth, anything is possible.* There is no limit to what God can do. However, we can limit His work in us through our unbelief. We need to pray that God will restore to His Church a greater understanding of the power of the Truth—the power that is in Jesus—and the power and authority that is given to us because He has imparted that truth to us.

Chapter 9 of Matthew records several encounters people had with Jesus that emphasize the importance of faith and its connection to the truth.

FAITH AND FORGIVENESS

The first of these involved a paralyzed man who needed healing. That was not all he needed, however:

Some men brought to Him a paralytic, lying on a mat. When Jesus saw their faith, He said to the paralytic, "Take heart, son; your sins are forgiven." At this, some of the teachers of the law said to themselves, "This fellow is blaspheming!" Knowing their thoughts, Jesus said, "Why do you entertain evil thoughts in your hearts? Which is easier: to say, 'Your sins are forgiven,' or to say, 'Get up and walk'? But so that you may know that the Son of Man has authority on earth to forgive sins...." Then He said to the paralytic, "Get up, take your mat and go home." And the man got up and went home. When the crowd saw this, they were filled with awe; and they praised God, who had given such authority to men (Matthew 9:2-8).

Jesus responded to the faith He saw in the paralytic and the men who had brought him by telling the paralytic that his sins were forgiven. Wait a minute! Hadn't the man come for healing?

Undoubtedly. Why then the talk of forgiveness of sins? Apparently, the paralytic's condition made it so that he could not speak for himself, but Jesus saw into his heart and knew what he really needed. Forgiveness was the first step toward the healing that followed.

Of course, Jesus' statement about forgiving sins immediately offended the critics and the teachers of the law who were observing the scene. A mere man claiming to forgive sins would indeed be blasphemy, and this is how they viewed Jesus. They understood that He was equating Himself with God, but they did not believe Him. Jesus called their unbelief "evil thoughts," then challenged them by asking which was easier, to tell a crippled man that his sins were forgiven or to tell him to get up and walk. This was not merely an academic question; it cut to the very heart of who Jesus was. Only God has the power to heal miraculously and only God has the authority to forgive sins. A healing miracle by Jesus was thus also proof of His power to grant forgiveness of sins.

For some reason we tend to think that forgiveness is easier than healing. Perhaps this is because we have more faith for forgiveness than we do for healing. After all, the forgiveness of sins is a central theme of the Christian faith, whereas healing has been sidelined in the teaching of the Church for much of her history, at least until the present century. *If we exercised as much faith for healing as we do for the forgiveness of sins, we would see far more people healed, delivered, and set free from the bondages in their lives.* The reason is simple: Jesus, the Truth, overcomes sin *and* sickness with equal ease. Neither is more difficult than the other. It is as easy for Him to heal as it is for Him to forgive.

Jesus proved this by healing the paralytic. From Matthew's perspective it was a simple, matter-of-fact event. Jesus said to the paralytic, "Get up, take your mat and go home." The man got up and went home. Just like that. The outcome was never in doubt. As a result, Jesus' critics were silenced and God was glorified (not to mention the forever-changed life and eternal destiny of the former paralytic).

FAITH AND FOLLOWING THE TRUTH

Matthew next recounts an event that must have been a vivid memory for him: his personal call to follow Jesus. The call of Matthew is a clear demonstration of the fact that God does not look at things the way men do. As a tax collector, Matthew would not have been anyone's choice for anything. Tax collectors were among the most-hated groups of people in the land. Servants of the Roman occupation government, they were considered traitors to their nation. In addition, they had a widespread (and probably well-earned) reputation for dishonesty, greed, and corruption. Aside from collecting taxes for Rome, they lined their own pockets by overcharging and cheating the people. Who in his right mind would choose someone from this despised group for a holy calling?

Yet that is exactly what Jesus did. According to Matthew himself:

As Jesus went on from there, He saw a man named Matthew sitting at the tax collector's booth. "Follow Me," He told him, and Matthew got up and followed Him. While Jesus was having dinner at Matthew's house, many tax collectors and "sinners" came and ate with Him and His disciples. When the Pharisees saw this, they asked His disciples, "Why does your teacher eat with tax collectors and 'sinners'?" On hearing this, Jesus said, "It is not the healthy who need a doctor, but the sick. But go and learn what this means: 'I desire mercy, not sacrifice.' For I have not come to call the righteous, but sinners" (Matthew 9:9-13).

We do not know how much contact, if any, Matthew had with Jesus before this. In any event, there must have been something very compelling about Jesus because Matthew immediately left his occupation and followed Him. Jesus challenged Matthew to leave his greed, fraud, deception, and sinful past and come follow the truth, walk in the truth, and be set free by the truth. For Matthew it was an irresistible invitation.

Matthew's life was forever changed the day he put his faith in the Truth. Likewise, all of us who have trusted in Christ have seen our lives transformed, whether dramatically or more gradually over a period of time. Whatever our individual experiences, none of us are the same persons we were before we met Jesus. The truth has already impacted us to a considerable degree. We do not think the way we used to; we do not have the same priorities or the same standards for living. There may still be many areas that need to be changed by the power of God, but He is already at work, progressively making us more and more like Jesus. What He has begun He will complete (see Phil. 1:6). His desire is that *we* desire to see our lives in line with the truth. *The more we believe the truth and the more our lives are submitted to the truth, the greater will be the faith, authority, and power of God that can flow through our lives.*

This passage also reveals some insight into the mind of Jesus. He said that He had "not come to call the righteous, but sinners." To reach sinners, Jesus had to go where they were, and He did not hesitate to do so, even when it meant violating social convention. In fact, He actively sought them out in order to lead them to the truth. Matthew is a perfect example.

Faith Reaching Out

Matthew next records three examples of people reaching out in faith to Jesus and having the truth transform the circumstances of their lives: a Jewish synagogue leader, a woman with a hemorrhage, and two blind men. In each case the miracle is directly related to the faith of the recipient.

1. *A Jewish Synagogue Leader*

...a ruler came and knelt before Him and said, "My daughter has just died. But come and put Your hand on her, and she will live." Jesus got up and went with him, and so did His disciples. ... When Jesus entered the ruler's house and saw the flute players and the noisy crowd, He said, "Go away. The girl is not dead but asleep." But they laughed at Him. After the crowd had been put outside, He went in and took the girl by the hand, and she got up. News of this spread through all that region (Matthew 9:18-19,23-26).

From the parallel accounts of this story in the other Gospels we know that the "ruler" who came to Jesus was named Jairus and that he was a leader in the synagogue. What kind of faith did it take for this man to *believe* that Jesus could raise to life his dead daughter? How many of us exercise that kind of faith? Apparently Jairus harbored no doubts. His words are confident: "Come and put Your hand on her, and she will live." Faith takes different forms with different people. In Matthew 8:8, the centurion's faith required only the spoken word of Jesus for healing. Jairus was different. His faith needed the physical presence and touch of Jesus. Each exercised faith in a different way, and Jesus responded accordingly. Jesus always responds to the precise nature of the faith that has been put in Him. He meets us where we are and, as we follow Him and allow our faith to grow, He leads us to where He wants us to be: into heights of spiritual reality we never dreamed possible.

Jesus entered Jairus' house amidst the loud wails of lament from the professional mourners and others gathered there. The assembled crowd laughed at Jesus when He told them that the girl was not dead but asleep. It is not uncommon to be laughed at for believing the truth rather than the circumstances. Jesus was unaffected by their laughter, however. He understood something they didn't: Death is only a fact; it is not the truth. Jesus, He who is the Resurrection and the Life, was going to speak the truth of life over the fact of the young girl's death. Her return to life was as certain as a sleeping person's return to wakefulness. He knew that she would rise from the dead because He had seen the faith of her father to believe, and God always honors that kind of faith.

Jesus put the noisy, skeptical crowd outside. God doesn't want spectators; He wants men and women of faith to stand together and to believe together. From the parallel accounts we know that only the girl's parents were with Jesus when He raised her. Jesus simply took her by the hand and she got up. That was it. No hype, no fanfare; just the truth coming against negative circumstances and transforming them into something wondrous and joyous. *The truth overcame death itself.* What Jesus did for that young girl He made possible for all of us through His death and resurrection. Life from death is our inheritance as believers.

2. *The Woman With a Hemorrhage*

Just then a woman who had been subject to bleeding for twelve years came up behind Him and touched the edge of His cloak. She said to herself, "If I only touch His cloak, I will be healed." Jesus turned and saw her. "Take heart, daughter," He said, "your faith has healed you." And the woman was healed from that moment (Matthew 9:20-22).

While Jesus was on His way to Jairus' house He was met by a woman who had suffered bleeding for 12 years. From the parallel accounts in Mark and Luke we know that she had spent a great deal of money on doctors and medicine, but could not be healed. Now, with Jesus nearby, she pressed through the crowd. All she wanted to do was touch Him. Her faith told her that one touch, even of Jesus' garment, would be enough to heal her. If she could only touch the Truth, the Truth would set her free.

The woman's faith was rewarded. She touched the edge of Jesus' cloak and was instantly and completely healed. Jesus then made a very interesting statement. He said, "Take heart, daughter, *your faith has healed you.*" I've heard so many preachers and others say that faith cannot heal. That's the exact opposite of what Jesus said to this woman. "*Your faith has healed you.*" Jesus knew what He was talking about. If He had meant "God healed you," or "I healed you," He would have said so. Instead, He said, "Your faith has healed you." It couldn't be any clearer.

This woman placed her faith in Jesus as the Truth through whom she could be healed. In effect, Jesus was saying, "*Your faith in Me, your faith in the Truth, has healed you.*" The inference is that without that faith she would not have been healed. Imagine her joy after 12 years of sickness! Like her, many people today need to believe that they can touch the Truth and be changed. He is just as close now as He was then. He is as close as our hearts and our Bibles. The Truth is always accessible to us.

3. *Two Blind Men*

As Jesus went on from there, two blind men followed Him, calling out, "Have mercy on us, Son of David!" When He had gone indoors, the blind men came to Him, and He asked them, "Do you believe that I am able to do this?" "Yes, Lord," they replied. Then He touched their eyes and said, "According to your faith will it be done to you"; and their sight was restored (Matthew 9:27-30a).

When two blind men sought out Jesus for healing, He didn't ask them how long they had been blind, what the cause of their blindness was, whether they were in good standing with God, or whether or not they were in right relationship with others. He didn't ask if they had confessed their sin or were walking in righteousness. He just asked this simple question: "Do you believe?" The implication is that their healing depended on their reply. When they answered, "Yes, Lord," He touched their eyes and they were healed. *Faith is the key that releases the power of the truth of God into our circumstances.*

SPEAKING THE TRUTH IN FAITH

Sometimes it really amazes me that in the face of the clear power, presence, and activity of God such as we have seen in these encounters (and in what we see happening so much today) that anyone could fail to believe. Yet it happens all the time. That just shows the depth and power of spiritual blindness and the deception of the enemy. Even in the midst of a great work, Jesus had His critics:

> *...a man who was demon-possessed and could not talk was brought to Jesus. And when the demon was driven out, the man who had been mute spoke. The crowd was amazed and said, "Nothing like this has ever been seen in Israel." But the Pharisees said, "It is by the prince of demons that He drives out demons"* (Matthew 9:32-34).

Notice the two distinctly different, even opposite, reactions to Jesus' actions in this case. The ordinary people marveled at the miracle and, although this is not stated, probably praised God as the source of the work. The miracles that Jesus performed always pointed to the power and glory of the Father. The Pharisees, on the other hand, offered only criticism and accusation. These men were not stupid. They were among the most highly educated in the land. No one knew the law and the religious teachings better than they. Certainly they knew, even more than the common people, that the works that Jesus did were possible only by the power of God. Yet their hatred of Jesus and their hostility to His ministry caused them to publicly attribute the mighty work of God to satan. They knew better. Talk about blasphemy! It was tantamount to saying that God was in league with the devil! What was worse, these were probably some of the same men who earlier had accused Jesus of blasphemy when He pronounced the forgiveness of sins for the paralytic. This simply shows that, no matter how much proof and evidence are available, when someone doesn't *want* to believe, he *won't* believe.

I remember on one occasion visiting a young boy in a hospital who had suffered an accident and had been in a coma for several days. The doctors were very perplexed and concerned. The boy was lying in a ward all by himself. I went in and just stood by his bedside for a few minutes, praying for his healing. Apparently, just after I left the hospital, the boy woke up. No one was expecting him to regain consciousness, so there were no nurses or attendants around. The boy was found simply wandering around the hospital, perfectly well. The medical staff quickly rushed him back to bed because they thought that he shouldn't be up and about after being in a coma for so long. They even tried to sedate him, but he didn't respond to it. He was completely healed. Everyone was amazed. When I went to meet his family and told them what had happened, they simply said to me, "Isn't it wonderful what doctors can do?" They knew as well as I that the doctors hadn't been able to do anything to help the boy. God had performed a miracle. Nevertheless, if you don't *want* to believe, then you *won't* believe.

One of the most difficult things for us as Christians is to speak the truth in faith over our lives when we are fighting sickness. There is a great temptation to concentrate on the problem and the need; to focus on the symptoms and the circumstances. This is important because we place our lives under our words, and when we talk about the problem we place our lives under the problem. Too often, we like to talk about our needs and problems so that we can elicit sympathy and pity from other people. When we are having a hard time we want everybody to know it so that they will feel sorry for us.

Can you imagine Jesus doing that? Can you picture Jesus sitting down with His disciples and saying, "Peter, John, I don't know how I'm going to put up with this any longer. There was more opposition today. The Pharisees were after Me again. They are persecuting Me. I feel so hurt, so damaged. Every time I come to Jerusalem it is the same thing: rejection and abuse. I need healing of My memories. Would you pray for Me?" The very idea is preposterous. Jesus would never have done that. He always used the shield of faith to quench the fiery darts of the evil one. He always spoke the word of truth that overcame the opposition. Is it too much to believe that we can do the same?

It is not always easy to speak the truth. Someone asks us how we are doing, and we say, "Well, by the stripes of Jesus I'm healed." Immediately they want to know how we are *really* doing. We need to be consistent and persistent in speaking the truth in faith over our situation. That doesn't necessarily mean always quoting Scripture, but whatever we say needs to be consistent with the truth. Paul tells us that we have Christ in us, the hope of glory (see Col. 1:27). If Christ is in us, cannot His word be spoken through us? Cannot the truth come forth from our mouths? Can we not walk in that truth and continue in that truth until we see the truth prevail in that situation? Jesus teaches us to persevere and that he who perseveres to the end will receive a reward (see Mt. 10:22). Respond to the truth of Jesus with faith. Persevere in faith. Speak the truth in faith over the problems in your life and watch how the overcoming power of God changes your circumstances. Keep all your conversation in line with the truth. To speak about the problem again and again confirms your faith in the problem. Continually speaking the truth demonstrates your faith to overcome the need; not using faith slogans, but speaking the truth from the heart.

Your prayer and your conversation with others should not be at variance, for that would be double-mindedness. What you believe in the prayer room you need to speak also at other times. There is little point in saying, "Jesus, I believe Your promises. I believe that I have received what I have asked for," only to tell someone else, "It seems to be a pretty hopeless situation."

Jesus says that the double-minded are unstable and cannot expect to receive anything from the Lord (see Jas. 1:7-8). Remember, Jesus listens to your thoughts from the moment you wake up to the time you fall asleep. So you can't fool Him by saying you believe when you do not.

So what can you do if you know you are not in a place of faith concerning a particular situation? Don't try to bluff your way through with God. Be honest with Him. Confess your unbelief and ask for His forgiveness. Then begin to pray and speak His words of truth over the circumstances. He will remind you of what *He* says about the situation.

Faith is simply agreeing with what God says; seeing things as He sees them. *Persevering in faith is holding onto His words, despite your feelings, fear, the opinions of others, or the lies of the enemy.*

Chapter Five

Taught by the Presence

While Jesus was with them, the disciples could encounter His Presence physically. They were living and walking with the Truth. The prospect of His going away left them devastated and grief-stricken.

Jesus explained, however, that His departure was for their good. The truth that was with them would be *in* them once the Holy Spirit had come to fill their lives. He promised His disciples that He would ask the Father to "give you another Counselor to be with you forever—the Spirit of truth…" (Jn. 14:16b-17a).

The Holy Spirit would continue the ministry of Jesus within those who believed in Him. At the Last Supper, Jesus taught the disciples how He would do this. Until this time, Jesus had spoken very little about the Holy Spirit. Now, the disciples would need to understand the part He was to play in their lives. Jesus taught them: "…The world cannot accept Him, because it neither sees Him nor knows Him" (Jn. 14:17a). This was the gift of God to those who believe in Jesus.

"But the Counselor, the Holy Spirit, whom the Father will send in My name, will teach you all things and will remind you of everything I have said to you" (Jn. 14:26). It is not the Spirit's purpose to initiate, but to remind the disciples of *all* that Jesus said, the Spirit and the Word working together in their lives.

"When the Counselor comes, whom I will send to you from the Father, the Spirit of truth who goes out from the Father, He will testify about Me" (Jn. 15:26). He will not only remind the disciples of what Jesus said, but He will also declare who Jesus is and what Jesus has done. This will enable the disciples in their turn to testify about Jesus (see Jn. 15:27).

"But when He, the Spirit of truth, comes, He will guide you into all truth. He will not speak on His own; He will speak only what He hears, and He will tell you what is yet to come. He will bring glory to Me by taking from what is Mine and making it known to you" (Jn. 16:13-14). The Spirit of Truth will not act independently of the Father and the Son. He will speak to the believer what He hears from Heaven, so that the believer knows both God's leading and enabling in his life.

One statement after another identifies the Holy Spirit as the Spirit of Truth. The Holy Spirit of Truth is our Counselor—another one of the same kind as Jesus—who is with us forever. The Greek word for "Counselor" is *parakletos*, which means "intercessor," "advocate," or "comforter." It is the noun form of the verb *parakaleo*, which means "to call near" or "to call alongside." The Holy Spirit, then, is one who has been "called alongside" us as our Counselor, Intercessor, Comforter, and Teacher. These words reveal a personal relationship of warmth and intimacy.

Jesus was the *first* counselor, the "Wonderful Counselor" spoken of in Isaiah 9:6. *Another* Counselor, the Holy Spirit, was necessary for the disciples because Jesus was returning to the Father. Up until then, the disciples had seen the Spirit operating in Jesus; now He would be living *in them*. That would make all the difference to the disciples; the Holy Spirit would not simply be *with* them, He would be *in* them.

THE HOLY SPIRIT IS PART OF THE TRIUNE GOD

The Bible plainly teaches that God relates to man in three distinct Persons: Father, Son, and Holy Spirit. They are *all* God and all *the same* in essence, nature, and being: *one* God manifesting Himself in *three* distinct Persons. Perhaps the clearest scriptural illustration of this truth is found in the accounts of Jesus' baptism. Jesus comes up out of the water, the Spirit descends upon Him in the form of a dove, and the Father speaks from Heaven, "This is My beloved Son, in whom I am well pleased" (see Mt. 3:16-17 KJV).

Some people seem to believe that we must have separate relationships with the Father, the Son, and the Holy Spirit. I think this is a mistaken way to look at our relationship with God. We have to take it as a matter of faith: If we know one, we know all three; if we have a relationship with one, we have a relationship with all three. Jesus told His disciples, "If you really knew Me, you would know My Father as well. From now on, you do know Him and have seen Him. ...Anyone who has seen Me has seen the Father..." (Jn. 14:7,9). If we know Jesus, then it is through the life and power of the Holy Spirit living within us; and if we know Jesus, then we know the Father. We can't have a relationship with Jesus without having a relationship with the Holy Spirit and with the Father.

Sometimes in the course of our spiritual growth as believers, it seems as if our focus is more on the Person and ministry of one than the other two. For example, sometimes God will lead us to concentrate more on the ministry of the Holy Spirit, and we learn more about the Spirit and His Presence and work in our lives. The Spirit has always been there, ever since we became believers, but now we are coming to know Him in a deeper way than before. We may receive the baptism of the Spirit and a fresh anointing and see a greater release of the Spirit's activity in our lives. This may cause us to feel that we know the Holy Spirit much more, when in reality we are simply seeing more of His activity in our lives than before.

At other times, we will be led to focus on Jesus and the meaning of what He did for us on the cross; and at still others, on the Father and His love, mercy, and grace and His over-ruling sovereignty as the Almighty. What God is doing is helping us to know *Him* by leading us to better understand how He relates to us as Father, Son, *and* Holy Spirit. *We live and walk as **children** of the Father, as **brothers** and **joint-heirs** with the Son, and as **temples** of the Holy Spirit, who sanctifies us and pours His rivers of living water out of us.* We need all three of these dynamics working in our lives at all times. We relate to the Father because He is the source of Truth, to the Son because He is the Truth who died that we may know the Truth and be set free by it, and to the Spirit who fills us with the Truth so that we are ambassadors of Truth in the world.

THE HOLY SPIRIT TESTIFIES ABOUT JESUS

One of the key ministries of the Holy Spirit in our lives is to focus our thoughts, our words, our witness, and our ministries squarely on Jesus. If we are led by the Spirit, we will say and do only those things that the Spirit tells us, and He will tell us only those things that He has received from the Son. This is the way Jesus Himself operated in His own ministry. Even though He was the Word of God made flesh who lived among us, He never acted on His own initiative. He always submitted to the Father, doing only what He saw the Father doing, speaking only the words the Father gave Him to speak. Jesus' ministry on earth really revealed what the *Father* was saying and doing. In the same manner, God's call to us as believers, and to His Church, is to reveal what *Jesus* is saying and doing. The Holy Spirit within us focuses us upon Jesus so that we reveal Him, the Light of Truth who shines brightly in a dark world blinded by sin, deception, and unbelief.

The Spirit and the Word work together in harmony and unity. That is very important. If we focus on either one to the neglect of the other, we will become unbalanced in our understanding. Emphasizing the Spirit without solid grounding in the Word can lead to freakish excess, while concentrating on the Word and ignoring the Spirit can result in legalistic bondage. When the two operate in harmony, however, people are set free and walk in freedom.

The Holy Spirit testifies about Jesus, not about Himself. Jesus told His disciples, "When the Counselor comes, whom I will send to you from the Father, the Spirit of truth who goes out from the Father, He will testify about Me" (Jn. 15:26). Nowhere in the Scriptures do we find a single example of believers preaching about the Holy Spirit. The subject of the gospel was Jesus Christ. At Pentecost Peter referred to the events taking place as the fulfillment of God's promise to pour out His Spirit on all flesh, but he preached Jesus (see Acts 2:14-36).

The believers preached in the *power* of the Holy Spirit, but they *proclaimed* Jesus. The Holy Spirit is the promise of God given to those who place their faith in Jesus. He indwells, teaches, and guides believers and empowers us to do the work of the Kingdom of God. The whole thrust of New Testament preaching was Jesus, and that is still true today. People need to hear the message of Jesus. When they place their faith in Jesus, they are born again of the Spirit, and the Spirit comes to dwell within them. Jesus is the way of salvation to everyone who believes. The Spirit is the gift of God to everyone who believes.

The Holy Spirit also glorifies Jesus. Speaking of the Holy Spirit, Jesus said, "He will bring glory to Me by taking from what is Mine and making it known to you" (Jn. 16:14). The Spirit has no interest in bringing glory to Himself. That is not His purpose. Even in Heaven worship is the *activity* of the Holy Spirit. Wherever the Spirit of God is in control, Jesus will be glorified.

If we attend a meeting or hear a preacher speak and everything is "the Spirit this and the Spirit that," and Jesus is pushed into the background, that is a sure indication that the flesh has taken over. How would you relate to a preacher who came along and simply talked about all the great things he did? You would say he was only glorifying himself and his ministry and it would be a big turn-off. However, if he came and talked about all the great things Jesus had done and was doing, you would say that he was a great man of God because he was giving all the glory to Jesus. That is exactly what the Spirit does. He does not speak on His own initiative, nor does He draw attention to Himself. He speaks only what He has been given to speak and reveals what He has been given to reveal. The Holy Spirit is not an exhibitionist but a revealer, and He reveals Jesus.

THE HOLY SPIRIT GUIDES US INTO ALL THE TRUTH

Another ministry of the Holy Spirit is to help us understand the truth. Jesus said, "But when He, the Spirit of truth, comes, He will guide you into all truth. He will not speak on His own; He will speak only what He hears, and He will tell you what is yet to come" (Jn. 16:13). *The Spirit never acts independently of the Father and the Son. He listens to the Father in order to reveal the Son.* So even when we are not listening, the Holy Spirit is listening. That is why it is always good to pray in the spirit. Paul said that "he who speaks in a tongue edifies himself" (1 Cor. 14:4a), which means that the Spirit speaks what Heaven tells Him to speak over our lives and our circumstances and into the situation about which we are praying. To make this work, we have to cooperate with what the Spirit is doing in us. We have to walk with Him, allowing Him to work through us so the rivers of living water flow out of us.

The Holy Spirit guides us into all the truth both by reminding us of all the things Jesus told us and by helping us understand what they mean. Jesus said, "But the Counselor, the Holy Spirit, whom the Father will send in My name, will teach you all things and will remind you of everything I have said to you" (Jn. 14:26). The Spirit's function in this regard is not selective. He does not choose only certain truths that we may want to hear; His job is to remind us of *all* of them. Some of the things Jesus said about discipleship and the cost of following Him, for example, are hard truths to accept and follow. We would much rather concentrate on such things as the miraculous, on the signs and wonders and the exciting promises that Jesus made. As much as we might like to, the Spirit will not let us escape from even the most difficult things Jesus said. If Jesus said them, then they are true and we need to listen to them.

In His role as teacher and guide, the Spirit does not give us the luxury of being selective about what we will hear and receive. Everything Jesus said is significant. If we are going to be the revival people whom God wants us to be, every aspect of what Jesus said needs to be reflected in our lives personally and in the Church corporately. The Holy Spirit not only declares those truths in us but also enables them. *The Holy Spirit then is not only the Spirit of Truth who reminds us of things, but also the power of God who enables us to do the things that He brings to our minds. As He declares, He enables.*

In between the Spirit's declaring and enabling lies our response. Without our response there will be no enabling. Many people hear, but if they don't respond, they won't be enabled to act. The Church has often been guilty of hearing but not doing, which is why James says, "Do not merely listen to the word, and so deceive yourselves. Do what it says" (Jas. 1:22). God will always enable us when we respond. That response may sometimes involve repentance, but it always involves faith to believe what He says and to step out in obedience. As we move in obedience the Holy Spirit enables us to do that which He has revealed to us.

THE HOLY SPIRIT CONVICTS THE WORLD OF SIN, RIGHTEOUSNESS, AND JUDGMENT

We have focused so far on ministries of the Spirit that apply mainly to individual believers and churches. The Holy Spirit also is at work in the world. Jesus explained the role of the Spirit in the world this way:

When He comes, He will convict the world of guilt in regard to sin and righteousness and judgment: in regard to sin, because men do not believe in Me; in regard to righteousness, because I am going to the Father, where you can see Me no longer; and in regard to judgment, because the prince of this world now stands condemned (John 16:8-11).

The Holy Spirit was sent to indwell *believers*, yet His presence will "convict the world of guilt." This means that as believers, we are the principal channels of the activity and ministry of the Holy Spirit of Truth in the world. So if the Holy Spirit is flowing in our lives in the way that God intends, the world will be convicted of sin, righteousness, and judgment. This is exactly what happens during times of revival. The reason it doesn't happen more often is because the Church wants to keep the Holy Spirit experiences for itself. We want to receive for our own sake, to meet our own needs, whereas Jesus said that the Spirit was given for the sake of the world.

The Holy Spirit was given in order to convict the world of sin, righteousness, and judgment. What happens when the Spirit convicts of sin? First of all, there is a new or heightened awareness of sin and its seriousness. All of us who have become believers have experienced this. Under Holy Spirit conviction, sin, once ignored, becomes a serious matter that must be dealt with. There is a deep sense of guilt before God and of the need for forgiveness. Sin conviction puts in the heart of a sinner the awareness of his need for God.

Awareness of sin should lead to repentance—the deliberate choice to turn away from sin and turn to God—and confession of faith in Christ. Of course this is possible only if the message of Christ is being proclaimed. No one can be converted without the activity of the Holy Spirit. The entire process of conversion is a work of the Spirit but He often uses us to bring it about. People are not going to get convicted or converted through our wisdom or through our testimony alone, but through the activity of the Holy Spirit. Wherever we go, the Spirit goes with us and can work through us to bring about conviction and conversion.

The Holy Spirit also convicts the world with regard to righteousness. As soon as we are made aware of our sin, we become aware of our need for righteousness. The problem is that we have no righteousness of our own. There is no way we can attain a righteous standing before God in our own merit or effort. However, Jesus is our righteousness. He is our salvation. Salvation isn't something that we have. Salvation is a person: Jesus. His name even means "Yahweh is salvation." When we become rightly related to Jesus, who is salvation, we enter a state of righteousness based on His merit as the sinless Son of God. We live constantly in His saving grace and in His righteousness because we live in right relationship with Him.

Jesus' coming gave mankind a standard of righteousness that is forever the measuring stick by which God judges the world. That standard is on display also in the changed, surrendered lives of believers who are living and walking in the truth. Conviction with regard to righteousness comes as those in the world see the standard of Christ before them and recognize how far short of that standard they fall. God's ideal desire is for the world to see the righteousness of Christ lived out in the lives of the redeemed, leading to conviction and conversion.

Jesus said also that the Holy Spirit would convict the world "in regard to judgment, because the prince of this world now stands condemned." The Holy Spirit brings awareness of what Jesus has done in regard to the enemy. Jesus overcame the devil time and again throughout His life, being tempted "in every way, just as we are—yet was without sin" (Heb. 4:15b). The Holy Spirit focuses on the victory of Jesus and brings awareness that He who is in us is greater than he who is in the world (see 1 Jn. 4:4). In other words, *if we have the Spirit of Christ, we have the Spirit of victory. He has overcome, so we are able to overcome.* All who overcome will receive the crown of life.

The Holy Spirit Gives Us
the Fullness of Life in Christ

Another ministry that the Holy Spirit does for us is make known to us the things of Christ. Jesus said, "He will bring glory to Me by taking from what is Mine and making it known to you. All that belongs to the Father is Mine. That is why I said the Spirit will take from what is Mine and make it known to you" (Jn. 16:14-15). Jesus is saying:

All that belongs to the Father belongs to Jesus.
All that belongs to Jesus is revealed to His followers
    by the Spirit.
All that the Spirit reveals becomes ours.

Isn't that wonderful? This is what Paul means when he says, "Praise be to the God and Father of our Lord Jesus

Christ, who has blessed us in the heavenly realms with every spiritual blessing in Christ" (Eph. 1:3). God has blessed us in Christ with fullness of life. Jesus said, "I have come that they may have life, and have it to the full" (Jn. 10:10b).

The fullness of God's life is in us *right now*. We don't have to wait for it or make payments on an installment plan. We have it right now as a present reality. We are complete in Christ. He has given us everything we need to prepare us for eternity. Remember Paul's words, "Christ in you, the hope of glory" (Col. 1:27b).The Holy Spirit in us reminds us that we are in Christ and are complete in Him.

Why did God give us His Spirit? It was so that we could know that we know God. John wrote in his first letter, "We know that we live in Him and He in us, because He has given us of His Spirit" (1 Jn. 4:13). In Him "we live and move and have our being" (see Acts 17:28) and we know that He is in us and we in Him. This fullness of life we have is possible only through the power and operation of the Holy Spirit within us. None of what we have would be available to us without Him.

Chapter Six

Empowered by His Presence

Truth is powerful because Jesus is the Truth, the very Word of God. The Word spoken brought the universe into being. The Word in the flesh brought freedom from sin, defeat of death, and eternal life to all who believe. The Word in the Spirit gives wisdom, authority, and freedom to all who walk in the truth.

Truth has a power that neither comes from the world nor is understood by the world because outside of Jesus there is no truth in the world. The world lives on facts and confuses those facts with truth. Facts are worldly and temporal while truth is spiritual and eternal. Spiritual truth cannot be understood by non-spiritual means. Paul explained this to the Corinthians when he wrote:

We have not received the spirit of the world but the Spirit who is from God, that we may understand what God has freely given us. This is what we speak, not in words taught us by human wisdom but in words taught by the Spirit, expressing spiritual truths in spiritual words. The man without the Spirit does not accept the things that come from the Spirit of God, for they are foolishness to him, and he cannot understand them, because they are spiritually discerned (1 Corinthians 2:12-14).

Lost people—those "without the Spirit"—cannot understand spiritual things because they lack spiritual insight, which only comes through the Presence of the Spirit of God. It is not God's desire for people to remain in spiritual darkness, however. He wants everyone to know Him. When writing to Timothy, Paul described God as one "who wants all men to be saved and to come to a knowledge of the truth" (1 Tim. 2:4).

How is a lost world to be brought to a "knowledge of the truth"? God's plan is for the world to come to know Him through the lives and ministries of believers. *As followers and disciples of Christ we are witnesses to the transforming power of the truth.* We know from personal experience how Christ has brought us from death to life, from fear to faith, and from hopelessness to assurance. The same power that transformed us can transform the world. That power—the same power that Jesus exercised on earth and that raised Him from the dead—resides in us through the Holy Spirit. We are to walk boldly in the truth; to let our light shine in such a way that lost people will see in us evidence of the Truth beyond themselves and be drawn to Him.

POWER FOR FREEDOM

Freedom is the hallmark of Christians. There are no slaves in God's household; we are all free children in His family. Paul wrote to the Corinthians, "Now the Lord is the Spirit, and where the Spirit of the Lord is, there is freedom" (2 Cor. 3:17), and to the Galatians, "It is for freedom that Christ has set us free. Stand firm, then, and do not let yourselves be burdened again by a yoke of slavery" (Gal. 5:1). Notice the tense of the verbs: "there *is* freedom"; "Christ *has set* us free." The *truth* of our lives is that we are free to walk in the "glorious freedom of the children of God" (Rom. 8:21). Too often, however, we allow the *facts* of our lives—our troubles, problems, sicknesses, discouragements, etc.—to put us in bondage to the attitudes and mind-set of the world.

God wants all of us to walk in the freedom we have in Christ. All around us are people in bondage who need to see the freedom we walk in so that they too can be set free. The truth has the power to set people free from any bondage that enslaves them: sin, ignorance, hatred, fear, sickness, spiritual blindness, even death. Bondage of any kind contradicts the truth and goes against the will and purpose of Jesus. The truth that brings freedom is revealed in the teaching and example of Jesus:

> *To the Jews who had believed Him, Jesus said, "If you hold to My teaching, you are really My disciples. Then you will know the truth, and the truth will set you free." ...I tell you the truth, everyone who sins is a slave to sin. Now a slave has no permanent place in the family, but a son belongs to it forever. So if the Son sets you free, you will be free indeed"* (John 8:31-32,34-36).

The key to freedom is not the truth alone, but *knowledge* of the truth. *It is the truth we **know** that sets us free.* We learn that truth by "holding to" the teachings of Jesus; by obeying them and making them our own. That is the mark of a disciple. We walk in freedom when we learn to believe and speak the truth over every area of our lives so that the things the enemy uses to attack us cannot prevail and overcome us. The power to overcome resides in us through the Holy Spirit, and no earthly power can withstand that power. Jesus told His disciples, "In this world you will have trouble. But take heart! I have overcome the world" (Jn. 16:33b).

Christ has already given us everything we need to live a life of victory. *The same power and authority that were His in overcoming the world are ours as well.* We have authority to "overcome all the power of the enemy" so that nothing can harm us (Lk. 10:19). We have the keys of the Kingdom of Heaven so that whatever we bind on earth is bound in Heaven and whatever we loose on earth is loosed in Heaven (see Mt. 16:19). Literally, the Greek means that whatever we bind on earth is *already* bound in Heaven; what we loose on earth is *already* loosed in Heaven. This means that we have the power and authority to prevent on earth whatever Heaven prevents and to release on earth whatever Heaven releases. Our position before God as believers is one of great authority and privilege. It also carries great responsibility. We must exercise our authority in submission to Christ for the building up of ourselves and others in faith and knowledge and in the experience of walking in the freedom of the Spirit.

POWER FOR SPIRITUAL WARFARE

It is very important that we understand the responsibilities we have for walking and remaining in freedom. Many Christians are quite familiar with the part of James 4:7 that says, "Resist the devil, and he will flee from you." That's a great promise, but sometimes we tend to overlook the first part of that verse: "Submit yourselves, then, to God." The order is important: *Submit* to God, then *resist* the devil. When we submit ourselves to God, we submit to His authority and that enables His authority to be exercised through us. *The devil flees because he cannot stand against such authority.* He has no power over us except what we allow him to have through disobedience to God, personal sin, or lack of faith.

These Scriptures and many others teach us that we each have the responsibility to bind and to loose, to overcome the enemy, to resist the devil in our own lives. It is not the responsibility of other believers to do it for us. For example, every person in the New Testament who was delivered from demonic powers was a nonbeliever at the time and was set free by Jesus or someone acting in His name. There is no evidence anywhere in the New Testament of any believer being delivered through the ministry of another believer. This is because every believer has the authority and the responsibility to resist the devil and all the powers of darkness for himself. Of course, we can agree together in prayer and that is powerful and effective. Matthew 18:19 promises that if two believers agree about anything they ask for, it will be done by the Father. We can come alongside another believer and stand with him in faith and add our authority to his in resisting the devil and his works, but it is not for any of us to do this on *behalf* of another believer.

If we want to help another believer be free from what binds him, we need to help him understand the power and authority *he* has been given by the Lord and that he needs to exercise them in faith, claiming his freedom in the name of Jesus. So we can lead him to the point where he himself is standing in faith, exercising his authority, resisting the evil one, and overcoming in the name of Jesus. If we try to do these things for him, he will never be equipped to deal with the wiles and temptations of the devil. *We need to build people up in the truth so they can walk in it themselves.*

The current rise in Christian counseling reveals that instead of walking by faith in the Lord Jesus Christ, many Christians have become counselor-dependent rather than God-dependent. They look to others to help them, fight for them, pray for them, and deliver them. This is not what the Lord wants for His children. *We must learn to take authority and stand with faith and confidence ourselves in our Christian walk.* Because He has already given us the power and authority, He wants us to exercise them in faith to overcome. As we obey Him we will begin to see His promises fulfilled in our lives. Remember that true faith is a matter of *doing*, not just of speaking. It is *obedience* rather than empty words.

Our authority in Christ is wide-ranging, covering every situation in which we might find ourselves. We are to speak and to act with His authority in every circumstance so that we live as victors rather than as victims. We are to bind whatever God wants to see prevented in our lives and release whatever God wants to see released. Sometimes we think we lack something and pray for God to supply it when all the time we have within us all the riches and resources He has already given us. When we are born again, we have the Kingdom of God within us, along with all the authority, riches, and resources that go with it. The Holy Spirit is living within us and we do not lack any spiritual gift. *We already have the fullness of life. We already have the authority to overcome the enemy. We are already complete in Him.* As we live in these truths, we draw upon the resources that God has already put within us and speak the life, power, healing, and victory of Jesus Christ over our circumstances. That is how the truth sets us free.

The Power of Speaking the Truth

The truth won't set us free if it is locked up inside us, however. It has to be released. We have to speak it over our lives with faith. If we speak the truth over our lives before problems arise, many of those problems will never take hold of us and put us into a negative position. It is good to speak health over our lives daily rather than waiting to get sick and then turning to the Lord to be our Healer. It is good to speak the love of God over our lives rather than waiting until we are in a spot where we are not acting in love and end up in some kind of bondage. It is good to speak the mercy of God over our lives to guard against resentment or unforgiveness that could put us in a perilous position in relation to God.

Jesus said, "For out of the overflow of the heart the mouth speaks. The good man brings good things out of the good stored up in him, and the evil man brings evil things out of the evil stored up in him" (Mt. 12:34b-35). Paul told the Corinthians, "It is written: 'I believed; therefore I have spoken.' With that same spirit of faith we also believe and therefore speak" (2 Cor. 4:13). Of whom is this written? God Himself believed and spoke creation into being. "Let there be light," He said, and there was light. Jesus spoke, "Be opened," and blind eyes were opened, deaf ears could hear, and dumb mouths could speak.

That same Spirit of faith is in you as a believer. You can speak things into being over your life and the lives of others around you. Notice, however, that this Spirit of faith gives you the ability to believe *before* you speak. Faith comes before words, and the words we speak reveal what is in our hearts. If our hearts are full of negativism and defeat, then that is what our words will reflect, and that is what will control our lives. Likewise, a heart full of faith, joy, and love will also be reflected in our words and will control our lives.

James likens the tongue to a rudder of a ship. It is only a small part, but it directs the course of the ship. Likewise with the tongue. Whatever you say will direct the course of your life. So when your speech disagrees with God's Word, you are at odds with Him; you have steered off course. When you direct the course of your life according to His words, you are at one with Him. Your life is on course.

Every time we speak, we make a choice and place our lives under that choice. If we speak of the problem, we place our lives under the problem. If we speak of the need, we place our lives under the need. If we speak of sickness, we place our lives under sickness. If we speak the truth, we place our lives under the truth. If we speak problems, need, or sickness over other people, we curse them. If we speak the truth over them, however, we bless them.

The Holy Spirit does not give you words of failure, criticism, or despair. He reminds you of the words of truth and urges you to speak accordingly. He wants you to speak the truth in love over your own life and the lives of others.

We have a responsibility to bring to people the word of truth that they need to build them up, to encourage them, and to draw from them the faith in Jesus that will enable them to have a fresh encounter with the Truth. They need to be taught how to build up a deposit of truth within themselves so that no matter what arises in their lives, they will respond to the situation with faith.

Here's an example. Two believers receive the exact same prognosis from their doctors: cancer that will kill them in three months. According to the doctors there is no hope. Nothing can be done. Surgery is not possible, and there is no other treatment that will help. The first believer listens to this gloomy forecast and goes home with two cancers, not one. The cancer in his body is a fact, but he also leaves with a cancer in his spirit because he has placed his life under the fact of his sickness. He may subsequently claim healing in Jesus' name and pray for God's healing grace to touch his life, but it will be a struggle for him. He will concentrate on getting the cancer out of his body without realizing that he has allowed it into his spirit.

The second believer refuses to put his life under his sickness. Instead, he speaks the truth in faith, saying, "In the name of Jesus, I will not die. I will live because Jesus is my healer. I believe that by the stripes of Jesus I am healed." Now this believer is not doubting the reality of the sickness and he will still need to see the evidence of the healing, but the difference is that he has not allowed the fact of his sickness to get into his spirit. His spirit is filled with the truth of God, so he takes the shield of faith against the arrow that is fired at him and with the sword of the Spirit immediately attacks the sickness with the word of faith.

Some time ago a woman told me that she had heard me use this illustration at a meeting she had attended about a year before. At the time she had no idea that three weeks later she would find herself in that exact situation. Her doctor told her that she had cancer and would die in a few months. Her immediate reaction was to panic, but then the Holy Spirit reminded her of my illustration. To her own astonishment she found herself turning to the doctor and saying, "Doctor, I'm a born-again Christian and I do not believe I will die of this disease, but that Jesus Christ will heal me." She did not deny the fact of her cancer, but she refused to believe in it. She went to her home group and asked them to pray. When she returned to the hospital a month later for her next examination there was no trace of the cancer. She was completely healed.

This woman had a deposit of truth and faith in her spirit so that when she was in a bad situation she was able to react with faith and see the truth overcome the fact. This is why *it is important to **build up** a deposit of truth and faith in our lives rather than wait until a crisis comes and then try to get faith in the middle of need.* A deposit of truth built up beforehand gives us the ability to counteract anything that comes against us, especially those things that come when we least expect them.

Jesus said, "Whoever believes in Me, as the Scripture has said, streams of living water will flow from within him" (Jn. 7:38). He was speaking of the Holy Spirit, who would produce rivers of living water that would flow from the innermost part of our being as believers: rivers of life, rivers of power, rivers of love, rivers of everything that is positive that comes from the Spirit of God. There is so much that we can speak and release that is good, powerful, and effective. We don't have to leave the ground to the enemy to fill with his negativity. We can fill the circumstances and the atmosphere around us with the truth of God. In order to do this, though, the truth must pervade our entire thought process; our hearts and minds must be full of the truth.

The Power of the Word

Filling our hearts and minds with the truth means that we must know the truth, and that is why it is important for us to be students of God's Word. Regular Bible study is essential for discipleship and for building up the deposit of truth that will enable us to pull down the strongholds of the enemy and overcome his attacks. *When we know the Word we can take Scriptures about our place in Christ and speak them regularly over our lives: Scriptures about health and healing and salvation; Scriptures about God's abundance and provision; Scriptures of joy and peace, love and grace, mercy and forgiveness.* God's Word is living, and when we speak it over our lives we release His Spirit and life over us.

We can also use the Word of God powerfully in prayer. Which are more powerful, our words or God's words? The answer should be obvious: God's words. That being the case, why not use God's words when we pray? I'm talking about more than simply praying in accordance with His Word; I mean actually using the words of Scripture in prayer.

While I was a pastor in the early 1970s our church experienced a wonderful move of God, particularly in the area of healing. For a period of about 15 months every sick person we prayed for was healed. That was a sovereign move of God's Spirit. During the same time He taught us a new way to pray. Eighteen different healing groups met for prayer every week. The prayers consisted solely of the words of Scripture and the names of those for whom we were praying. We learned first of all to claim for ourselves the spirit and life that were in those words by speaking pertinent Scriptures again and again. We then spoke those same words over the one we were praying for. It was like firing an artillery shell that exploded in that person's life with the power of God. We simply directed the Word of God toward those who needed to receive from Him.

This was not a mechanical repetition of Scripture. We believed that every time we spoke God's Word over a person's life, the healing power, the Spirit of life in those words, was impacting that person's life. We practiced this kind of prayer not only for healing, but for salvation as well. Some spoke Scriptures of salvation and the grace of God over the lives of unsaved family members and friends. Many were set free by the truth in this way as a result of prayer and became Christians.

Another way to use the Scriptures in prayer is to take a passage and pray the words of those verses over our own lives, over our churches, and over our cities and nations. This is a regular practice at Kingdom Faith Church where I am now senior pastor. For example, take this passage from Isaiah chapter 61:

> *The Spirit of the Sovereign Lord is on me, because the Lord has anointed me to preach good news to the poor. He has sent me to bind up the brokenhearted, to proclaim freedom for the captives and release from darkness for the prisoners, to proclaim the year of the Lord's favor...* (Isaiah 61:1-2).

We can pray this passage over our own lives just as it stands: "The Spirit of the Sovereign Lord is on *me*...the Lord has anointed *me*...He has sent *me*...." We can also pray it over our churches in a corporate sense: "The Spirit of the Sovereign Lord is upon *us*...the Lord has anointed *us*...He has sent *us*...." We can pray it over our city or nation: "The Lord has anointed *us* to preach good news to the poor *of this city*. He has sent *us* to bind up the brokenhearted *of this nation*...." Having prayed in such a manner, we can proceed with confidence, expecting God to move mightily in our church, city, or nation to carry out His Word. *Our confidence is based on the knowledge that by praying God's own words back to Him, we are praying in line with His Word and therefore in accordance with His will.*

Such prayer is very powerful and effective and can change the spiritual atmosphere not only in our personal lives, but in our churches as well. Once we get even a few people in our churches praying this way, something new will begin to happen. Hearts will be stirred within the church and the spiritual environment of the city will be changed. As more and more believers are stirred to pray, the spiritual atmosphere of the entire nation can be changed.

It is past time for us as God's people to realize the power and authority we have through taking the words of truth and speaking those truths over the nations. It is just as important that we learn to speak truth in *all* our conversation, not just our prayer times. It won't do much good to pray positive truths and then speak a lot of negativity over our lives, churches, cities, or nations. Our conversation should be in line with our prayer.

Of course, it is only from the overflow of the heart that the mouth speaks (see Mt. 12:34). If our hearts are full of negativity and judgment and despair and hopelessness, then that is what we will speak, and our prayers will be relatively ineffective. When we pray from hearts full of the truth, power, and life of the Word of God, however, then that truth, power, and life are released over those for whom we are praying.

The Power of Walking in the Truth

If only we would come to really understand the great power that God has made available to us through the truth! We need to become like Jesus: He thought the truth, spoke the truth, acted in the truth, related in the truth; He *was* (and is) the

Truth. Everything He did was within the perspective of the truth. God wants the same for each of us. He doesn't want us to turn to the truth only when we have a need or when we are in a tight spot. *He wants us to be filled with the truth and walk in it all the time so that it pours out of us like a river, causing us to have a powerful and positive effect wherever we go.* God's truth in us produces holiness and a greater awareness of His Presence and power. His grace, mercy, and love flow out of our lives to touch other people.

We teach the members of our church to see themselves as nation-changers. Every believer needs to see himself or herself as a nation-changer. If we will use the power and faith that God has given us, we can be significant in seeing God move and change the nations. The problem is that so many Christians look at themselves and feel so weak and impotent. It seems that local issues, not to mention national ones, are too big for them to handle. This is nothing more than a lack of faith. God wants us to have a faith big enough to see that He has given us the power and authority to make a difference; we can be leaven in the lump and salt for the earth and light for the world. We can be the city set on a hill that cannot be hidden. Let us in faith and confidence use the power and resources that God has made available to us. Let us lay hold of the tremendous resources that reside in the truth and let the river of truth pour out of us, enabling God's purposes to be fulfilled.

Chapter Seven

Saying "No" to the Presence

Just as believing the truth sets us free and has a powerful influence upon our lives and circumstances when we speak it in faith, so rejection of the truth has dire consequences. The Bible contains many warnings about this. Quite often, a warning against unbelief appears in conjunction with a promise of blessing for belief. A good example is found in the third chapter of John's Gospel:

> *For God so loved the world that He gave His one and only Son, that whoever believes in Him shall not perish but have eternal life. For God did not send His Son into the world to condemn the world, but to save the world through Him. Whoever believes in Him is not condemned, but whoever does not believe stands condemned already because he has not believed in the name of God's one and only Son* (John 3:16-18).

We are all familiar I'm sure with the wonderful promise in the sixteenth verse: eternal life for all who believe. Look at the warning in verse 18: Whoever does *not* believe *is condemned already*. Those who reject the truth are under the condemnation of God that pertains to all of sinful mankind. *Faith in the truth delivers us from that condemnation and brings us into the glorious liberty of the sons of God*, while rejection means spiritual darkness and the eternal judgment that our sins deserve.

Sadly, the truth is not received or accepted by everyone. The realities of a fallen, sin-darkened world raise many obstacles to understanding and receiving the truth. Jesus knew this to be so. He told His listeners, "Enter through the narrow gate. For wide is the gate and broad is the road that leads to destruction, and many enter through it. But small is the gate and narrow the road that leads to life, and only a few find it" (Mt. 7:13-14). He also offered hope when He said, "I have told you these things, so that in Me you may have peace. In this world you will have trouble. But take heart! I have overcome the world" (Jn. 16:33). We need to understand the obstacles to the truth so that we can guard against them in our own lives, and help others avoid them also.

The Obstacle of Deception

By its very nature deception is one of the most difficult obstacles to the truth. The reason is simple: People who are deceived honestly *believe* they know and are following the truth. In other words, you are deceived when you think you are right, but you are not!

Often you will have conflicting thoughts. You will ask yourself: "Is this the Lord speaking? Are these my own thoughts, or is the enemy trying to mislead me?" There is no sin in conflict. However, you make your choice as to which of these conflicting thoughts you believe when you speak! It is important, therefore, to choose to speak the truth, not something that approximates the truth. This will be especially true just before Christ returns. Paul wrote to the Thessalonians:

The coming of the lawless one will be in accordance with the work of Satan displayed in all kinds of counterfeit miracles, signs and wonders, and in every sort of evil that deceives those who are perishing. They perish because they refused to love the truth and so be saved. For this reason God sends them a powerful delusion so that they will believe the lie and so that all will be condemned who have not believed the truth but have delighted in wickedness (2 Thessalonians 2:9-12).

Many are deluded into believing a lie, having no deposit of truth in their hearts to give them discernment. Others reject the truth, deliberately choosing the way of sin and selfishness. Hating the truth, they delight in wickedness and therefore continue in darkness and condemnation.

There are still others who once knew and followed the truth but have wandered away from it into error because of carelessness or from being led astray by false teachers. Paul warned Timothy about two in particular when he wrote, "Among them are Hymenaeus and Philetus, who have wandered away from the truth. They say that the resurrection has already taken place, and they destroy the faith of some" (2 Tim. 2:17b-18). This is a good example of how deception often works: It begins with an element of truth, but distorts it until it means something else.

Sometimes people abandon the truth in favor of myths. They accept any kind of superstition, philosophy, or occultic belief that allows them to justify lifestyles and behavior that focus on themselves rather than upon the Lord Jesus Christ and His purposes. Therefore selfishness itself is a deception. These kind of people often look and sound religious, seeking churches or preachers who will tell them what they want to hear. Unfortunately, those kinds of churches and preachers are not very hard to find. There are many preachers who preach their own ideas rather than the Word of God. They water down the gospel to make it attractive and appealing to their hearers rather than confront them with the truth.

Deception is also widespread in the Body of Christ, which makes it all the more important for us to hold fast to the truth, to check what we hear against Scripture, and to know what we believe and why so we can be confident that we really are walking in the truth and not allowing ourselves to be deceived. John provides good counsel in his first letter:

> *Dear friends, do not believe every spirit, but test the spirits to see whether they are from God, because many false prophets have gone out into the world. This is how you can recognize the Spirit of God: Every spirit that acknowledges that Jesus Christ has come in the flesh is from God, but every spirit that does not acknowledge Jesus is not from God. This is the spirit of the antichrist, which you have heard is coming and even now is already in the world* (1 John 4:1-3).

One of satan's greatest deceptions with Christians is to get them to believe that as long as they think they have a valid interpretation of the Word of God (no matter what the Word actually says), that they must be walking in the truth. However, Scripture must be interpreted by Scripture. Many believers therefore are deceived into thinking that they are walking in the truth when in reality they are walking in their own ideas. How do we guard against this deception?

Paul gave excellent counsel to Timothy in this regard: "Do your best to present yourself to God as one approved, a workman who does not need to be ashamed and who correctly handles the word of truth" (2 Tim. 2:15). "Do your best" translates the Greek work *spoudazo*, which means to make effort, be diligent, to study. *There is **no substitute** for knowledge of the Word of God in guarding against deception.*

THE OBSTACLE OF UNBELIEF

One of the most challenging things Jesus ever said is found in John chapter 14: "I tell you the truth, anyone who has faith in Me will do what I have been doing. He will do even greater things than these, because I am going to the Father" (Jn. 14:12). I have read in books and actually heard preachers say that the "greater things" Jesus refers to here mean only the accumulated works of all believers. However, that is not what Jesus said. His words were, "*anyone* who has faith in Me" will do greater things than He because He was going to the Father. This verse strikes at the very issue of unbelief. This is what Jesus promises each individual believer.

Unbelief can cause us to water down the Word of God because of our inability to accept it at face value; to acknowledge that it means what it says. In this case, once we realize that Jesus was referring to the coming of the Holy Spirit, it is easy to understand why we can do greater things than Jesus. Apart from salvation itself, there is no greater work that God can do in our lives than to send the Holy Spirit to dwell within us. The holy God actually makes our bodies temples of His Spirit. That is something Jesus could not do during His earthly ministry because the Spirit could not be given until after Jesus was glorified (see Jn. 7:39). Because you have received the Spirit as an indwelling Presence, you can pray for others and God's Spirit will come and fill them. This is a greater work than Jesus could perform during His earthly ministry for the Spirit was not yet given, because Jesus was not yet glorified. So sometimes ignorance and a lack of understanding lie behind our unbelief, causing us to deny the truth in that area.

There is a disturbing tendency today for most people, including many Christians, to de-emphasize the teachings of Scripture in favor of more "modern" ideas and methods. For example, we know well that psychiatry cannot set people free in the way that Jesus Christ can. Yet we still cling to and insist on modern, man-derived techniques of psychological treatment while neglecting the counsel of Scripture. We need to renew our faith in God's Word; faith in Jesus, the Truth who is able to set people free. As long as we stick to God's Truth, we will see powerful and effective results. The moment we allow unbelief to turn us from God to the thoughts and ideas of men, we are headed for trouble.

In his second letter to Timothy, Paul referred to people who were "always learning but never able to acknowledge the truth" (2 Tim. 3:7), while others were "men of depraved minds, who, as far as the faith is concerned, are rejected" (2 Tim. 3:8b). Many times human intellect stands in the way of faith. That is not to say that faith is anti-intellectual, but people who regard human learning as the highest pinnacle of truth are rarely open to matters of faith. It is indeed in the mind where the battle so often takes place. *When God gives revelation of the truth, that comes right up against all our human and natural thinking.* We are then faced with the choice of whether to surrender our thinking to God's thinking or hold on to our own. Repentance, remember, is a change of mind; turning our thoughts over to God so that we come into line with His thoughts. Those who oppose the truth, Paul says, have depraved minds. Their minds are actually in opposition to the mind of Christ. *True* knowledge actually *begins* with God, and those who deny Him are fools. The Book of Proverbs says, "The fear of the Lord is the beginning of knowledge, but fools despise wisdom and discipline" (Prov. 1:7), and the psalmist says, "The fool says in his heart, 'There is no God' " (Ps. 14:1a).

A young man once accused me by saying, "The trouble with you people who believe the Bible is that you have such small minds." To this I replied, "The trouble with you people who do not believe the Bible is that you do not have minds that are big enough! I want a mind that believes the sick can be miraculously healed, the dead raised, and a multitude fed from a boy's picnic!"

THE OBSTACLE OF SPIRITUAL DARKNESS

One of the reasons so much of the world rejects the truth of Jesus is because the enemy has bound the world in spiritual darkness, a darkness that can be broken *only* by the light of that truth. It is a darkness characterized by blindness, ignorance, deception, unbelief, superstition, incomprehension, and confusion. In the first chapter of his Gospel John wrote: "The light shines in the darkness, but the darkness has not understood it" (Jn. 1:5). Later on he had this to say in his first epistle:

This is the message we have heard from Him and declare to you: God is light; in Him there is no darkness at all. If we claim to have fellowship with Him yet walk in the darkness, we lie and do not live by the truth. But if we walk in the light, as He is in the light, we have fellowship with one another, and the blood of Jesus, His Son, purifies us from all sin (1 John 1:5-7).

Here John makes it very clear that those who are Christians walk in the light as Jesus is in the light. What does he mean, though, by "walk in the darkness"? When we reject the light of God's Word we are walking in darkness. We live for ourselves rather than for Christ and others. It's rather difficult to fellowship with and relate to others while you're in the dark.

One of John's main points in this letter is that we can tell what our relationship with God is like by our relationships with other people. If we say we love God but do not love our brother, we are only deceiving ourselves. The truth is not in us and we continue to walk in darkness. If we truly love God, we will love our brother. Jesus said, "By this all men will know that you are My disciples, if you love one another" (Jn. 13:35).

Love, then, is a key to overcoming the obstacle of spiritual blindness. John goes on to say, "Whoever loves his brother lives in the light, and there is nothing in him to make him stumble" (1 Jn. 2:10). To walk in the truth, then, is to walk in love. To love God is to love our brother. To walk in the light is to be at one with God and at one with our brother. *To live in the truth is to be in fellowship with the Father and the Son as well as with our Christian brothers and sisters.*

Truth is the light that shines into the darkness of our lives and brings revelation of God's will and purpose. As children of God we have been called to let the light of that truth shine before men in order to dispel the spiritual darkness in the world, so that people will see the glory of God in us and turn to Christ. That is why we must be very careful to walk in the light so that there is no spiritual darkness in our hearts; no deception or unbelief, no bitterness, hatred, or unforgiving spirit. Walking in the light means bringing our lives in line with the truth; bringing our thoughts, speech, actions, and relationships in line with God's Word. That is exactly what the Holy Spirit empowers us to do. He lives within us to make it possible. *We walk in the light as He is in the light, and through us He works to dispel the spiritual darkness in the world.*

THE OBSTACLE OF RELIGION

Jesus was surrounded all the time by enemies of the truth. His enemies were not the common people, the crowds who gathered to listen to Him. They were not enemies of the truth; they were simply ignorant of the truth. In fact, many of them, once they understood the truth, believed and followed Jesus. They were not the enemy. The enemies of the truth were the scribes and Pharisees, the respected religious leaders and experts in the law, and the Sadducees, the political/religious group who held a lock on the office of high priest. It was the leaders of religion who opposed Jesus most vigorously of all.

Why? Jesus' teachings and actions upset their tidy religious box with its form, ritual, and law. They thought they had the truth. They really believed that they were right.

Matthew 12:9-13 tells of Jesus healing a man in the synagogue on the Sabbath. To us this is no big deal; Jesus heals anytime, anywhere. To the Pharisees, however, it was anathema. According to their strict, legalistic, religious minds Jesus had violated the law against "working" on the Sabbath. They considered the law the ultimate truth. Jesus, however, *is* the ultimate Truth. He came "full of grace and truth" not to destroy the law, but to fulfill it. To the religious leaders He was a lawbreaker, and therefore under the judgment and condemnation of God.

The truth is an offense to many religious people. This is because "religion" is not interested so much in the truth as in *control*. Truth liberates. People caught in the bonds of legalistic religion fear freedom. They attack anything or anyone who threatens their comfortable world or narrow view of the "truth." That is why we should never be surprised when we face opposition for walking in the truth. Jesus said, "If the world hates you, keep in mind that it hated Me first. ...If they persecuted Me, they will persecute you also" (Jn. 15:18,20b). *If we are determined to hold fast to the truth, we will encounter opposition from the enemies of the truth, and many of those enemies will wear the garb of religion.*

When I speak of "religion" here, I mean a body of teaching and practice that focuses on tradition, ritual, and rules rather than on the condition of people's hearts before God or their relationship with Him. It is the kind of religion that Paul described as "having a form of godliness but denying its power" (2 Tim. 3:5a). Those who follow it will always oppose those who walk in the truth, because the truth exposes the lie and futility of empty religion.

The truth will always prevail. For that reason we must never compromise our faith in the Word—in the Truth—even in the face of opposition. Jesus never compromised. Someone might say that that's why He was crucified. That may be, but I would much rather hold fast to the truth and receive an eternal reward than to deny it and lose everything. Jesus said, "Whoever acknowledges Me before men, I will also acknowledge him before My Father in heaven. But whoever disowns Me before men, I will disown him before My Father in heaven" (Mt. 10:32-33). I don't want to be denied before the Father. I want to hold fast to the truth and be acknowledged by Jesus in Heaven. So I'm not going to compromise the truth just to go along with the crowd.

Unfortunately, even in the ranks of the Christian Church there are those who oppose the truth, either deliberately or because they are deceived. Remember the parable Jesus told about the wheat and the tares (see Mt. 13:24-30). A man sowed wheat in his field, and an enemy came at night and sowed weeds among the wheat. As the wheat and weeds grew together, the man's servants asked if they should pull up the weeds. He told them to let both grow together until the harvest, when the wheat would be gathered into the barns while the weeds were burned. In this story the wheat represents the children of God, the enemy is the devil, and the weeds are the children of the devil. The meaning is that the devil deliberately puts people who oppose the truth among those who believe the truth. That is why opposition to the truth so often comes from *within* the Church rather than from without.

Sometimes it isn't easy to tell who is "wheat" and who is "weeds" because the enemy is very subtle. Once we take a deliberate and firm stand for the truth, however, the picture becomes clearer. The character and hearts of people are revealed and sides are taken. It becomes much easier to distinguish those who hold fast to the truth from those who don't.

A word of caution is needed here. We must be very careful not to accuse or consider someone a "weed" who may in truth be a brother or sister in Christ who simply has a sincere and genuine difference of opinion with us. That is why Jesus said not to pull out the weeds. That will be done at the judgment by the only One qualified to do it: Christ Himself. In the meantime, *we must stand firm in the truth, trusting the Lord to honor His Word and advance His purposes and will through us in spite of opposition.*

THE OBSTACLE OF TRADITION

Another obstacle to the truth that is often closely linked to religion is tradition. Jesus challenged the Pharisees frequently on this very issue. Matthew recorded an instance in chapter 15 of his Gospel. The Pharisees challenged Jesus and accused His disciples of breaking the tradition of the elders by not washing their hands before they eat. Jesus responded with a counter-challenge: "And why do you break the command of God for the sake of your tradition?" (Mt. 15:3) He goes on to expose their practice of allowing a person to get around the commandment to honor his father and mother by committing as a "gift to God" whatever money he might otherwise be expected to use to help his aged parents. Jesus' charge in verse 6 is serious: "Thus you nullify the word of God for the sake of your tradition."

Tradition becomes a problem whenever it gets in the way of the truth. It is very easy for us to find our security in the familiar. The Pharisees loved tradition because they found their security in the known, the familiar, and in performing regular religious ritual. Faith, on the other hand, is a challenge. When we walk and live by faith we are reaching out all the time for God, expecting Him to do new things. We can't walk in the truth and stay in all the old ways and traditions of the past. Walking in the truth forces us to confront our feelings, our fears, our negative thought patterns, and the negative thoughts and ideas of the people and culture around us. We have to overcome those things daily with the truth spoken over our lives. *By confessing the truth of God we say no to the negative, limiting, and disheartening thoughts, ideas, and attitudes that the world tries to give us.*

The Obstacle of Hypocrisy

In the same chapter of Matthew where Jesus challenged the Pharisees concerning their tradition, He also challenged them concerning their hypocrisy, even citing the words of Scripture as evidence against them: "You hypocrites! Isaiah was right when he prophesied about you: 'These people honor Me with their lips, but their hearts are far from Me. They worship Me in vain; their teachings are but rules taught by men'" (Mt. 15:7-9). The word *hypocrite* comes from the Greek *hupokrites*, which refers to an actor playing a role. A related meaning is that of a pretender.

The Pharisees knew little and cared less about the state of their hearts before God. They trusted in the rules of the law and in their rituals and traditions, and valued the acclaim and respect of men more than the heart and mind of God. They were concerned about outward appearance rather than inward character. That is why Jesus likened them to whitewashed tombs:

> *Woe to you, teachers of the law and Pharisees, you hypocrites! You are like whitewashed tombs, which look beautiful on the outside but on the inside are full of dead men's bones and everything unclean. In the same way, on the outside you appear to people as righteous but on the inside you are full of hypocrisy and wickedness* (Matthew 23:27-28).

We can wear our nicest clothes, fix our hair just right, put a smile on our face, and even say all the correct "religious" words, and it all means nothing. It is what is on the inside that counts. There is no use cleaning the outside if on the inside we are full of negativity, unbelief, fear, failure, and defeat. We must let the light of the truth shine on us on the inside and allow the Spirit to clean out all the garbage, corruption, negativity, defeatism, and anything else that is contrary to God's desire.

The Pharisees' question about eating with unwashed hands gave Jesus the opportunity to make the point that uncleanness comes from inside a person, not from outside:

> *But the things that come out of the mouth come from the heart, and these make a man "unclean." For out of the heart come evil thoughts, murder, adultery, sexual immorality, theft, false testimony, slander. These are what make a man "unclean"; but eating with unwashed hands does not make him "unclean"* (Matthew 15:18-20).

We need to be careful to make sure that the person we are on the outside matches the person we are on the inside, and that both are motivated and enlightened by the truth. Our lives and behavior must match our words. Anything else is hypocrisy and a denial of the truth. Jesus said, "He who is not with Me is against Me" (Mt. 12:30a). Either we are with the truth or we are against it. There is no neutral ground.

God has given us the key of truth to unlock every door of opposition, but if we don't use the key, the door will stay shut. We will feel hemmed in by things that are facts, not truth. That can lead to feelings of depression, defeat, and failure. What we need is steady application of the truth to the facts and realities of our lives. God has provided a resource to make that possible. We will learn to apply and live the truth as we learn to listen to and obey the Holy Spirit who dwells in us for the purpose of leading us into the knowledge of the truth.

Chapter Eight

God in a Mirror

Whenever we encounter Jesus we encounter the Truth because He is the Truth. Whenever we encounter Jesus we encounter the Presence of God because He is God. Whenever we encounter the Presence of God we encounter the glory of God because His glory is linked to His Presence.

In times of renewal and revival, such as are occurring today in many places around the world, Christians acquire a heightened awareness of the Presence and majesty of God as He invades their lives in new dynamic and different ways. This experience quite often is accompanied by a deep sense of God's glory—His nearness; the weighty importance and awesomeness of His Person. No one who encounters God in this way is left unaffected.

When the original temple built by King Solomon in Jerusalem was dedicated, the glory of God descended in great power and sparked a national revival in the land. The event is recorded in Second Chronicles:

When Solomon finished praying, fire came down from heaven and consumed the burnt offering and the sacrifices, and the glory of the Lord filled the temple. The priests could not enter the temple of the Lord because the glory of the Lord filled it. When all the Israelites saw the fire coming down and the glory of the Lord above the temple, they knelt on the pavement with their faces to the ground, and they worshiped and gave thanks to the Lord, saying, "He is good; His love endures forever." Then the king and all the people offered sacrifices before the Lord. ... On the twenty-third day of the seventh month he sent the people to their homes, joyful and glad in heart for the good things the Lord had done for David and Solomon and for His people Israel (2 Chronicles 7:1-4,10).

There are several remarkable things about this account. First, the glory of God descended in response to the prayer of the king. Second, the presence of God's glory was so heavy and powerful that the priests could not enter the temple. Third, the sight of the fire and glory of God elicited praise and worship from all the people assembled. Fourth, the people received a deep awareness of God's goodness and love. Fifth, the effects of this encounter were lasting as the people, after an eight-day celebration, returned home "joyful and glad in heart" at the goodness of God.

When Isaiah encountered the truth of the glory of God, the result was holy fear, conviction of sin, cleansing from sin, and acceptance of his prophetic calling. The prophet records in Isaiah 6:1-8 that he was in the temple and "saw the Lord seated on a throne, high and exalted." Multitudes of seraphs flew back and forth, calling to each other, "Holy, holy, holy is the Lord Almighty; the whole earth is full of His glory." The noise was so thunderous that the whole temple shook and was filled with smoke. Isaiah cried out "Woe to me! I am ruined! For I am a man of unclean lips, and I live among a people of unclean lips, and my eyes have seen the King, the Lord Almighty." One of the seraphs then touched Isaiah's lips with a hot coal from the altar, saying, "Your guilt is taken away and your sin atoned for." Then Isaiah heard the voice of the Lord saying, "Whom shall I send? And who will go for us?" to which Isaiah responded, "Here am I. Send me!"

Isaiah's life was changed forever by his encounter with the glorious Presence of God. Seeing the infinite holiness and perfection of God brought home to him his own sinfulness and led him to cry out in confession. Receiving abundant grace and full forgiveness for his sins caused Isaiah to offer himself for God's use and service. One lesson from this is that when we encounter the Truth—the Presence, power, and glory of God—we are called on to make a response. We can either accept the truth or reject it. The one thing we cannot do is remain neutral.

GLORY AND THE OLD COVENANT

In Exodus 33:18, Moses makes a bold request of God: "Now show me Your glory." For any other man such a request might have been presumption, but for Moses it was a natural outgrowth of his relationship with God. Here was a man who had led a nation out of Egyptian bondage (under God's direction), brought them to the wilderness of Sinai, and passed on to them the law given to him by God. He had felt anguish and anger at the sin of the people as they so quickly forgot God and all His powerful acts on their behalf, turning instead to the worship of a golden calf, demonstrating by their actions a physical and spiritual desire to return to Egypt. Moses had interposed himself between the people and the wrath of God, interceding for them and turning away God's destructive judgment. Now God has instructed Moses to lead the people away from the Sinai area. Although He has promised to send an angel with them, God threatens not to go with them Himself, lest He destroy them on the way because of their rebellious nature (see Ex. 32:1–33:3).

For Moses, the thought of going without God's Presence was inconceivable. He not only wanted to experience the glory, he also wanted the glory to go with him. This was a man for whom the intimate Presence of God was a daily reality. Moses enjoyed a personal relationship with God that was at a level shared by very few in history (at least until the time of Christ) and by no others in his own day. Moses met God regularly at the "tent of meeting" set up some distance from the camp. A pillar of cloud would descend to the entrance to the tent as the Lord spoke to Moses. It was an intimate exchange: "The Lord would speak to Moses face to face, as a man speaks with his friend" (Ex. 33:11a). That's intimacy!

Moses' request to see God's glory was motivated by his desire for this continuing close Presence of God in his life:

> *"If You are pleased with me, teach me Your ways so I may know You and continue to find favor with You. Remember that this nation is Your people." The Lord replied, "My Presence will go with you, and I will give you rest." Then Moses said to Him, "If Your Presence does not go with us, do not send us up from here." ... And the Lord said to Moses, "I will do the very thing you have asked, because I am pleased with you and I know you by name." Then Moses said, "Now show me Your glory"* (Exodus 33:13-15,17-18).

God honors Moses' request, placing him in the cleft of a rock and covering him with His hand while His glory passes by. Moses is able to see only His back, because God had said, "You cannot see My face, for no one may see Me and live" (Ex. 33:20).

The Hebrew word for "glory" in verse 18 is *kabowd*, which has the basic meaning of being heavy in weight. It also came to mean to honor, or to give weight to another; to recognize that person's importance in the community. In reference to

God, it means His greatness and the splendor and weighty importance of His Presence among men. When Moses asked to see God's glory he was asking to see the unmistakable manifestation of God's Presence.

The glory of God's Presence was so great that it had lingering physical effects on Moses:

When Moses came down from Mount Sinai with the two tablets of the Testimony in his hands, he was not aware that his face was radiant because he had spoken with the Lord (Exodus 34:29).

Because of this, Moses wore a veil over his face between the times he went in to speak to God. He would remove it when he spoke to God, but when he came out to tell the people what God had said, they would see the radiance of his face and he would replace the veil.

The glory of the Lord revealed in this intimate and personal way was a rare occurrence under the Old Covenant, and it was experienced by only a few. The nation of Israel envisioned God's Presence as localized in the tabernacle and later in the temple. In their minds, the fortunes of the nation rose and fell on the Presence of God or the lack of His Presence. In First Samuel chapter 4, when the pregnant wife of the high priest Phinehas hears that the ark of the covenant has been captured by the Philistines and that her husband Phinehas and her father-in-law Eli are dead, the news sends her into labor. Just before dying from the strain of childbirth, she names her newborn son Ichabod, which means "the glory has departed," because she believed that with the capture of the ark, the glory of God had departed from Israel.

Although God has always been present with His people on earth, that Presence would take on a whole new meaning and dimension with the coming of Jesus and the institution of the New Covenant.

THE GLORY ON EARTH

Truth is a Person—Jesus—and He embodied the very Presence, power, nature, and glory of God. Paul made this clear in his letter to the Colossians:

> *He [Jesus] is the image of the invisible God, the first-born over all creation. ... For God was pleased to have all His fullness dwell in Him ... For in Christ all the fullness of the Deity lives in bodily form* (Colossians 1:15,19; 2:9).

John stated it just as plainly in the first chapter of his Gospel:

> *In the beginning was the Word, and the Word was with God, and the Word was God. He was with God in the beginning. ... The Word became flesh and made His dwelling among us. We have seen His glory, the glory of the One and Only, who came from the Father, full of grace and truth* (John 1:1-2,14).

This was something completely new. Never before had the Presence and glory of God resided on earth in such a tangible and accessible way. The Old Testament contains many references to the glory of God descending to the earth, such as at the dedication of Solomon's temple, or at Sinai when God gave the law to Moses, or when He led the people with a pillar of cloud by day and a pillar of fire by night. His Presence dwelled in the Holy of Holies in the tabernacle and later in the temple, approachable only by the high priest once a year on the Day of Atonement. Of course, the mind, heart, and providence of God have always been near and available to His people through prayer and obedience to His Word. *Not until Jesus came, however, was the Divine Presence so close, so tangible, and so immediately accessible to everyone who sought Him. Furthermore, through the Holy Spirit who now inhabits the*

hearts of believers, the Person of Christ and His glory is con-
tinually available as an indwelling Presence.

When John wrote, "We have seen His glory, the glory of the One and Only," he undoubtedly had in mind the unique experience he had shared with Peter and James when they had witnessed the transfiguration of Jesus. On that occasion Jesus had taken these three "inner circle" disciples with Him up on a high mountain where "He was transfigured before them. His face shone like the sun, and His clothes became as white as the light. Just then there appeared before them Moses and Elijah, talking with Jesus" (Mt. 17:2-3). The supernatural reality of this event was confirmed when they heard the voice of God from inside a bright cloud that enveloped them: "This is My Son, whom I love; with Him I am well pleased. Listen to Him!" (Mt. 17:5) John, James, and Peter witnessed a glimpse of the glory that Jesus had enjoyed in Heaven and would enjoy once again when He returned—a glory that was eternally His because of His divine nature.

Now that glory resided in flesh and blood, "full of grace and truth." Truth, grace, and glory were embodied in Jesus and dwelled among men. In fact, in John 1:14, the phrase "made His dwelling" translates the Greek word *skenoo*, which means to tent or encamp; to reside as God did in the ancient tabernacle. In other words, in Jesus the glory of God dwelled among men in the same way that He had dwelled in the tabernacle in the midst of the Israelite people.

What does all this mean for us? A couple of things. First of all, it means that in Jesus we have the clearest, most complete picture of God that we can ever have this side of Heaven. God wants us to *know* Him, and Jesus came so that we could. The second thing is that when Jesus told His disciples about His approaching death, He promised He would not abandon them. He told them, "And I will ask the Father, and He will give you another Counselor to be with you forever—the Spirit of truth"

(Jn. 14:16-17a). The English word *another* translates the Greek word *allos*, which means specifically "another of the same kind." The promised Holy Spirit would be "another of the same kind" as Jesus: the same in essence, nature, and character. Everything Jesus was the Spirit would be also. Just as the glory of God resided in Jesus, it would reside in the Spirit also. *The critical difference is that the glory would no longer be confined to a single body—Jesus—but would dwell as a* **real Presence** *through the Holy Spirit in the life of* **every** *believer.* There is no "ichabod." The glory did not depart when Jesus ascended. It is still here, inside every one of us who claims Christ as Savior and Lord.

Glory and the New Covenant

In his second letter to the Corinthians, Paul compares the ministry of the Old Covenant to that of the New, and reveals the fundamental difference between them in relation to the glory of God. Beginning in chapter 3 Paul writes:

> *Such confidence as this is ours through Christ before God. Not that we are competent in ourselves to claim anything for ourselves, but our competence comes from God. He has made us competent as ministers of a new covenant—not of the letter but of the Spirit; for the letter kills, but the Spirit gives life* (2 Corinthians 3:4-6).

God has made us competent. We need to believe that. We have no competence in ourselves: Jesus said that apart from Him we can do nothing (see Jn. 15:5). Through the Holy Spirit, however, we live in Him and He lives in us. He has made us competent as ministers of a new covenant, one that has nothing to do with legalistic "belief" in the truth or narrow focus on the minute details of absolute doctrinal precision and correctness, but is a dispensation of the Spirit. The Spirit of God confirms our faith in the truth by the way in which He moves in our lives and then is channeled through us, pouring out of us as rivers of living water. In practical terms, that means everybody around us gets wet with Jesus.

Paul continues in the next several verses to say that regardless of how glorious the ministry of the Old Covenant was, the ministry of the New Covenant in the Spirit is even more glorious:

> *If the ministry that condemns men is glorious, how much more glorious is the ministry that brings righteousness! For what was glorious has no glory now in comparison with the surpassing glory. And if what was fading away came with glory, how much greater is the glory of that which lasts!* (2 Corinthians 3:9-11)

Paul says that we have the "surpassing glory," the glory that lasts. In His great high priestly prayer recorded in John chapter 17, Jesus makes an amazing statement. After praying for all those who would come to believe through the teaching of the disciples, Jesus prayed, "I have given them the glory that You gave Me, that they may be one as We are one" (Jn. 17:22). *Jesus has given us the same glory that He was given by the Father! It is the surpassing glory that is greater than that of the Old Covenant, and it does not fade away*, as the radiance of Moses' face did. God wants that glory to shine in our lives, and that can happen only through the empowering of the Holy Spirit.

We have the glory! I have it and you have it. Where is it? It is locked up inside us somewhere and has to come out and be expressed in our lives. It is a glory that is greater than the glory that was upon Moses. When he met with God his face shone, but that glory gradually disappeared and he had to cover his face so that men wouldn't see it disappearing. There is a greater glory in us than the glory that Moses experienced, and God wants that glory to come forth and be seen by men.

So we have this ministry of God's glory. As Paul says, "And we, who with unveiled faces all reflect the Lord's glory, are being transformed into His likeness with ever-increasing glory, which comes from the Lord, who is the Spirit" (2 Cor. 3:18). There is no veil between us and God. The veil that existed under the Old Covenant was torn asunder when Jesus died on the cross, and we now have direct access to the Father. We can come with boldness and confidence before His throne of grace and there find mercy and grace "to help us in our time of need" (Heb. 4:16). We can reveal the glory of God through who we are and what we do because, with the veil taken away, we all reflect the Lord's glory.

Furthermore, we are being transformed into His likeness with ever-increasing glory. That means it is to become increasingly visible in our lives, being seen more and more in our actions, words, and character. This is impossible in our own strength. It must come through the Spirit of God. We need not only the Word of Truth but also the Spirit of Truth to impact our lives so that we can be the people of glory that God has called us to be.

Treasures in Jars of Clay

God wants the glory in us to shine in the world as a light shines in the darkness and dispels it. Continuing his letter to the Corinthians Paul writes:

> *For God, who said, "Let light shine out of darkness," made His light shine in our hearts to give us the light of the knowledge of the glory of God in the face of Christ. But we have this treasure in jars of clay to show that this all-surpassing power is from God and not from us* (2 Corinthians 4:6-7).

When God spoke at creation and said, "Let there be light," there was light. God looked on the light and saw that it was good. Why? Jesus, the Word, had gone forth from His mouth and brought into being exactly what God the Father had intended. Jesus spoke into being the things that were not seen. He said, "Be open," and blind eyes were opened and deaf ears were opened and dumb mouths were opened. He said, "Get up and walk," and the paralyzed and the crippled got up and walked. He said, "Peace, be still," and the storm was stilled.

God has made His light to shine in our hearts. Do you realize what that means? God has spoken over our lives and has said, "Let light shine out of darkness." *He didn't simply say, let the light shine **into** our darkness, or to let the light come and set us free from darkness, but that the light should shine **out** of us.* This is why Jesus says, "Let your light shine before men, that they may see your good deeds and praise your Father in heaven" (Mt. 5:16). God has prepared good things for us to walk in; not just the good things that we receive from Him but also the good things that He wants to accomplish through us so that His light shines out of us the way He intends. *His light in our hearts will give us "the light of the knowledge of the glory of God in the face of Christ" so that His glory can radiate out of us.*

Why then don't we see more of that glory being manifested in the lives of individual Christians and the corporate Church? Paul says that we have this treasure—this light of the knowledge of the glory of God in the face of Christ—in jars of clay. That means it is contained in our human bodies of flesh and blood. This is to "show that this all-surpassing power is from God and not from us." It is not something we must strive to possess. We already have it. There is a power within us that surpasses anything and everything else. So what is the problem? Why don't we see more evidence of His power in believers? It is because of our jars. Our treasure is concealed in jars of clay. We all know how much easier it is to concentrate upon the jar of clay rather than on the treasure that is inside it. We get so concerned about the jar—the shape of the jar, the happiness of the jar—that we forget what is inside.

How many of you, when you go to the supermarket, shop for the most attractive jars? Of course not. You know what you want and buy for *contents*, not *container*. God doesn't love us because of the way we look; He accepts us because of what He has put into us. Jesus is our righteousness, our holiness, our new identity. We are in Him and He is in us. We have no acceptance apart from Jesus; no place before God apart from Him. Outside of Him we have no righteousness. All that we are in godly terms is because we are in Him and He is in us: treasure in jars of clay.

Before we can really see the will and purpose of God fulfilled in our lives, we have to be more concerned about the treasure than we are about the jar. In fact, usually the jar has to be *broken* before the treasure can really be revealed in the way that God desires. That's why Paul says that "death is at work in us, but life is at work in you" (2 Cor. 4:12). The jars are being broken. Life is at work in us. We die to ourselves (broken jars of clay) so that the treasure (the life, power, Presence, and glory of God) pours out of us to impart life to others, causing us to be fruitful.

THE HOLY SPIRIT SANCTIFIES US

The glory and holiness of God belong together. When Jesus was praying His great high priestly prayer recorded in John chapter 17, He asked the Father regarding His disciples, "Sanctify them by the truth; Your word is truth" (Jn. 17:17). The word *sanctification* refers to something or someone "set apart" for God's use and involves holiness. *The Holy Spirit lives within us in order to make us holy.* He is transforming us, as Paul says, "into His likeness with ever-increasing glory, which comes from the Lord, who is the Spirit" (2 Cor. 3:18b).

How does the Holy Spirit sanctify us? Do we wake up one morning feeling holier than we were the day before? It doesn't work that way at all. When we cooperate with Him, the Holy Spirit brings us day by day more and more in line with the Word of God in our thoughts, character, actions, and words. This conforming to the image of Christ is impossible by our own effort. It is an exclusive work of the Spirit. All of us can remember times when we have tried to do or be what we think God wants, only to fail utterly because we tried to do it in our own strength. The Holy Spirit takes us into the Word and declares the things of Jesus to us. Next comes our response, and then His enabling that makes us more like Jesus. This is a lifelong process after we become believers.

Let's think about sanctification for a moment. We know that Jesus is our holiness, but we also know that holiness is something that has to be out worked in our lives. That involves two things: the putting off of anything that is unholy and the putting on of things that are holy. The Holy Spirit accomplishes the first by taking us into the Word and convicting us of both the unholy things in our lives as well as the holy and righteous things that should be in our lives but aren't. For example, He may convict us at the point of not being loving enough, or giving enough. When we respond in confession and repentance, telling the Lord that we want to change in those areas, the Spirit enables us to do it. So, little by little, we are becoming more like Jesus. We won't experience the change, we won't receive the enabling, though, until we step out in faith and obedience.

This brings us to a positive view of holiness. Holiness is not simply the absence of sin. It is not going around in sackcloth and ashes with long faces either. Very simply, *holiness is Christ-likeness.* Holiness, then, is really the fullness of life we have already talked about. If we are full of the Holy Spirit, we are going to live the fullness of life. That means *we will be full of love, full of joy, full of grace, full of mercy, full of forgiveness, full of power, full of peace, and full of faith.* Just as Jesus was full of all these things, so will we be full.

Now the sanctifying work of the Holy Spirit is to see more and more of that fullness in our lives so that rivers of living water are pouring out of us. Remember that when Jesus speaks of the Holy Spirit, He speaks of what flows out as well as what flows in. So Jesus prayed, "Sanctify them by the truth; Your word is truth" (Jn. 17:17). A couple of verses later He said, "For them I sanctify Myself, that they too may be truly sanctified" (Jn. 17:19). In other words, we can only be sanctified because Jesus offered His life totally without reservation. Because of Jesus' giving Himself totally to the will of the Father, the Spirit can perform His sanctifying work in us, fulfilling Paul's admonition:

> *Therefore, I urge you, brothers, in view of God's mercy, to offer your bodies as living sacrifices, holy and pleasing to God—this is your spiritual act of worship. Do not conform any longer to the pattern of this world, but be transformed by the renewing of your mind. Then you will be able to test and approve what God's will is—His good, pleasing and perfect will* (Romans 12:1-2).

How does this sanctification work in practical terms? Let me describe it this way. The Holy Spirit is just a little voice inside us that says "Give!" when we don't want to, "Love!" when we would like to turn the other way, and "Bless!" when all we really want to do is clobber the other person. *The Holy Spirit is God in us.* Sometimes in our flesh we want to scream out against being the person whom God wants us to be, but *the Holy Spirit is always there reminding us of what Jesus would do, what He would say, what He would think, what He would pray, what He would believe.* The proper relationship with the Holy Spirit is when we listen and take notice of Him because He is God's voice within us, and as we obey His voice, we find ourselves becoming more and more like Jesus.

So what is holiness? Holiness is living in perfect faith, perfect love, and perfect obedience. Praise God that we have the perfect One within us. I don't know how He puts up with us sometimes, but He does. He is infinite in His patience with us. When we fail, He doesn't condemn us. He forgives, restores, and says, "Walk in My truth and trust Me!"

Rest assured that God always finishes what He starts. All of us as believers are reconstruction projects in progress. The Holy Spirit will not stop until He has brought us into full maturity in Christ. He will never remove His Presence from us. Paul stated it this way:

...He who began a good work in you will carry it on to completion until the day of Christ Jesus (Philippians 1:6).

This, then, is our aim if we are going to live in His Presence through the power of the Spirit of Truth. In one situation after another you can ask yourself, "If Jesus were in this situation, what would He do? Well, that's what I need to do (in the power of His Spirit). What would He believe? That's what I need to believe. What would He say? That's what I need to say. How would Jesus pray? That's how I am to pray in His name!"

That is practical holiness, and you have the Holy One within you to enable you to live that way. And when you do so, the glory of God will be revealed through you—that glory that is inside you because Christ lives in you.

The Lord had purpose in revealing His glory to Moses. He wanted to release His people from bondage. He wanted a holy people for Himself. He had purpose in revealing His glory to Isaiah and to Peter, James, and John. And He has a definite purpose in placing His glory in you. He wants to release you from every bondage, so you can be one of His holy, "set apart" children, who can reveal His glory to others.

Chapter Nine

Captured by the Presence

In chapter 14 of his Gospel, John records an amazing statement by Jesus: "If anyone loves Me, he will obey My teaching. My Father will love him, and We will come to him and make Our home with him" (Jn. 14:23). Those who love Jesus will obey Him and will be loved by the Father. There is nothing new about that. Obedience is proof of love. It is the next part of the verse that is so incredible that it would be impossible to believe if it were not part of the Scriptures: "We will come to him and make Our home with him."

Wait a minute! Isn't it the Holy Spirit who comes to live in us? Yes, but God is not divided; He is One. If we have the Spirit, then we have the Father and the Son as well. Jesus said, "Anyone who has seen Me has seen the Father" (Jn. 14:9b), and "I am in the Father and the Father is in Me" (Jn. 14:11b). What an incredible thought, that God Himself dwells inside us as believers! Each of us is a temple, a dwelling place for the Trinity!

Of course this does not mean that God no longer resides in Heaven. It does mean that in a very real way, a supernatural way that we cannot fully comprehend, He resides *in* us. John wrote at the beginning of his Gospel, "The Word became flesh and made His dwelling among us" (Jn. 1:14a). In the person of Jesus, God dwelled for a time *among* us. The coming of the Holy Spirit brought about a fundamental change. Now, instead of simply dwelling *among* us, God dwells *in* us. There is a big difference.

Because He dwells in us, all the resources of God Himself are immediately available to us, conditional upon our obedience and submission to His will. Remember that Jesus' authority to work and act came from His submission to the will and authority of His Father. Jesus demonstrated power and authority in His life because He walked in perfect obedience to the Father's will. The same principle applies to us. *Power for living the Christian life comes as we walk in obedience.*

Likewise, failure to obey is a sign of lack of love. In the very next verse Jesus says, "He who does not love Me will not obey My teaching" (Jn. 14:24a). Disobedience essentially is selfishness: loving ourselves more than we love God and putting our desires ahead of His. We make the choice between obedience or disobedience, and the choice we make reveals the condition of our heart. At the center of it all lies the issue of abiding in Christ.

THE VINE AND THE BRANCHES

Jesus taught His disciples the concept of abiding in Him by using the illustration of a vine. Grapevines for producing wine were very common in Jesus' day, so it would have been a very familiar image. Jesus talked first about the functions and relationships between the vine and its branches:

I am the true vine, and My Father is the gardener. He cuts off every branch in Me that bears no fruit, while every branch that does bear fruit He prunes so that it will be even more fruitful. ... Remain in Me, and I will remain in you. No branch can bear fruit by itself; it must remain in the vine. Neither can you bear fruit unless you remain in Me. I am the vine; you are the branches. If a man remains in Me and I in him, he will bear much fruit; apart from Me you can do nothing. If anyone does not remain in Me, he is like a branch that is thrown away and withers; such branches are picked up, thrown into the fire and burned (John 15:1-2,4-6).

A vine consists of many different parts: the root system, the main stem, the branches, the leaves, and the fruit. Jesus didn't say, "I am the stem," or "I am the root system"; He said, "I am the vine." In other words, He is the *whole thing*: root, stem, branches, leaves, and fruit. We, however, are the branches. That means that we are part of Him. His life is in us and we cannot live apart from Him any more than a branch can live separated from the vine. The life in the branches comes from the vine. Just as life-giving sap flows from the vine into the branches, so life from the Spirit flows into us.

There are two kinds of branches: natural branches and those that are grafted in. Paul used this analogy when he wrote to the Romans about God's bringing Gentiles into the faith. The Jews were the natural branches because they were the original covenant people, while the Gentiles were the grafted branches because the covenant was extended to them later. Paul referred to the Jews in their rejection of Christ as natural branches that were "broken off because of unbelief" (Rom. 11:20b) and the Gentile believers as "a wild olive shoot" that had been "grafted in among the others" and now shared the "nourishing sap from the olive root" (Rom. 11:17). A few verses later he speaks of God as the one who both cuts off the natural branches and grafts on the "wild" ones. In addition, Paul says that God is able to graft back in those natural branches who turn away from their unbelief.

The purpose of the branches of the vine is to bear fruit; they are of no use for anything else. Vine branches have thin bark and are full of liquid sap—the life of the vine. Healthy branches produce abundant fruit because they are channels for the sap that gives them life. Unhealthy branches produce little or no fruit because something has interrupted the proper flow of the sap. Fruitless branches take life out but do not produce anything. That is why they are cut off.

If Jesus is the vine, His Father is the gardener who cuts off every fruitless branch and prunes every fruitful branch. The purpose of pruning is to increase fruitfulness. Cutting back the old growth leads to new growth. So pruning is always followed by a period of growth. If we are fruitful in our lives, growing in Christ and bearing fruit for His Kingdom, we can expect to go through periods when He prunes us. Pruning may be painful or costly at the time, but the rewards of greater fruitfulness will far outweigh whatever pain or cost we endure. *The time of pruning will result in new growth: more effective fruitfulness than we had before.*

So we can't get away from the pruning even if we are fruitful. It is an expression not only of God's ownership of us but also of His fatherly love. The Book of Proverbs says, "The Lord disciplines those He loves, as a father the son he delights in" (Prov. 3:12). That verse could be paraphrased, "The Lord prunes those He loves, as a gardener the vine he takes pride in." Pruning also serves to shape the branches so that they will grow in the direction and manner that the gardener desires. So we should neither fear nor despair over the "pruning" periods in our lives. They are a necessary part of God's preparing us for greater growth and more abundant fruitfulness.

Vine branches also tend to bear a lot of leaves. Plenty of lush green leaves can look really pretty and healthy, but too many of them hinder the bearing of fruit. This is because all the life and goodness of the vine is going into leaf production rather than fruit production. The leaves must be pruned back as well. There are a lot of Christians who are proud of their big, showy "leaves" of knowledge and gifts, but who have little fruit to show from their lives. They are not abiding in the truth. They may "know" the truth—they may have a mental understanding of words, doctrines, and concepts—but they are not living the truth, or allowing it to flow in them or through them. When we live the truth, our lives will bear the fruit. God will prune out everything that is not consistent with the truth.

The Father will prune out of your life whatever does not bring Him glory. He does not deal with every issue at once; He has a program of reform for you! However, you will be much happier without those things, and more of His glory will be revealed through the new growth and increased fruitfulness that follow.

Remain in the Vine

In John 15:4 Jesus says, "Remain in Me, and I will remain in you." The tense of the Greek word *meno* (remain) here indicates continuous action: "*Keep on remaining* in Me and I will *keep on remaining* in you." The very fact that Jesus gives us this command implies that we have a choice. We can *choose* whether or not to remain in Him. This has nothing to do with choosing to remain saved; that was taken care of once and for all when we believed. Rather, it means choosing to remain in the truth; choosing to continue to align our lives with the truth; choosing to abide in His Presence. Even though Jesus has commanded us to remain in Him, it is not inevitable that we will. If we love Him, we will remain in Him, because those who love Him obey Him, and obedience means remaining in Him by being obedient.

By remaining in Jesus we can bear fruit; apart from Him we can do nothing. What is the fruit that we will bear? For one thing, we will experience the freedom that comes from knowing the truth. We will know the joy of walking in the glorious liberty of the sons of God. And if the truth continues in you, what's going to be the fruit? You will witness the growth of Christ-like character in your life and an ever-deepening love and passion for God in your heart. Your ministry in the power of the Holy Spirit will mature in your service toward other believers and the lost. *Your driving desire will be that God be glorified in everything you do, say, and think.*

We cannot produce the fruit ourselves. Our function is to *bear* the fruit that is produced by the life of the vine in us. Divine life is creative by nature; fruit is an inevitable result. Our fruitfulness as Christians depends on the degree to which we allow the divine life of God to flow in us. This requires two important qualities of character: *humility* ("Apart from You, Lord, I can do nothing"), and *surrender* ("Not my will, Lord, but Yours be done"). The Word of Truth and the Spirit of Truth operate together to produce these things in our lives. In humility we acknowledge that it is the Lord, not us, doing the work, and in surrender we open ourselves so that He can display His fruit in our lives.

Jesus says in John 15:5b, "If a man remains in Me and I in him, he will bear much fruit." It is inevitable. The Holy Spirit speaks the truth to us. We cooperate and that truth bears fruit in our lives. It is the combination of the Spirit's voice and our response: *The Spirit speaks, we obey, the Spirit works.* He enables us to be the fruitful people God wants us to be.

I have the privilege of preaching in some of the major revival churches in Argentina, churches with tens, even hundreds of thousands of believers. What amazes me every time I visit these churches is the directness of the faith of the people and the quality of their love. To them living in revival is a very simple matter: You listen to the Holy Spirit and do what He says. God does the rest!

You see, the Holy Spirit will never tell you to do something that will not work in practice. Jesus does not lead a procession of failure, but of triumph. So His Spirit will tell you what to do so that you can overcome difficulties and be fruitful for God every day of your life.

If we humble ourselves and surrender to Him, we will be fruitful, and He will answer our prayers. Consider Jesus' words:

If you remain in Me and My words remain in you, ask whatever you wish, and it will be given you. This is to My Father's glory, that you bear much fruit, showing yourselves to be My disciples (John 15:7-8).

If we are living in the truth and the truth is living in us, then we will ask only for that which is in accordance with the truth. Jesus promised that anything we ask for in that manner will be given to us. This calls for faith and obedience. From God's perspective, there is no difference: *True faith is obedience.* James said that we are to be *doers* of the Word and not hearers only, that faith without works is dead, and that genuine faith will inspire and be demonstrated by good works (see Jas. 1:22; 2:17-18 KJV). *Faith leads to obedience, obedience leads to fruitfulness, and fruitfulness brings glory to God and shows the world that we are His disciples.*

REMAIN IN CHRIST'S LOVE

Another part of remaining in Jesus is to remain in His love. Once again, this is accomplished through obedience. The result will be joy. Jesus said:

As the Father has loved Me, so have I loved you. Now remain in My love. If you obey My commands, you will remain in My love, just as I have obeyed My Father's

*commands and remain in His love. I have told you this
so that My joy may be in you and that your joy may be
complete* (John 15:9-11).

Jesus is not only the Truth; He also is love. Living in the
truth then does not mean living according to a series of concepts or a corpus of teaching that God has placed before us.
Living in truth and love means living in Christ. Jesus said, "As
the Father has loved Me, so have I loved you." How has the
Father loved Jesus? It was directly related to Jesus' submission
to His Father:

*The reason My Father loves Me is that I lay down My
life—only to take it up again. No one takes it from Me,
but I lay it down of My own accord. I have authority to
lay it down and authority to take it up again. This command I received from My Father* (John 10:17-18).

If the reason the Father loved Jesus is because Jesus laid
down His life, and Jesus loves us the same way, then the reason Jesus loves us is because we also lay down our lives. What
this means in practical terms is that we do not live for ourselves. We are not selfish branches, hoarding all the life and
goodness and fruit and hiding it away somewhere for our
exclusive use. Instead, we live to bear fruit for the glory of the
Father. Have you ever seen a branch eating its own fruit?

How do we remain in Christ's love? As with everything
else, the key is obedience. If we obey His commands we will
remain in His love. Can you see how *true* love and *true* faith
involve *action*? It is not enough to talk about them. Their gen-
uineness will be proven by what we *do*. Now, we can't *earn*
the Father's love or a place in His Kingdom. We do not do
good works in order *to be* saved; *we do good works because
we **have been** saved. The presence of genuine love and faith
will be revealed by their fruit displayed in our lives.*

Obedience leads to the fullness of joy because when we obey there is no tension between us and God. Disobedience grieves and quenches the Spirit. Don't forget that God dwells in us through the Holy Spirit. We all know what it is like to live with someone whom we are at odds with. There is tension in the home. Whenever we are living in disobedience to the Lord there is tension within us because we are the temples of His dwelling. If we are abiding in the truth and cooperating with the Spirit, He will make us aware of areas of disobedience, which we will confess and repent. That way, complete fellowship is maintained. There is nothing hindering the flow of divine life in us and consequently we are filled with joy. Disobedience grieves the Lord; obedience reveals His glory.

LOVE ONE ANOTHER

Remaining in Christ's love is necessary for the fulfillment of Jesus' next command, that His disciples love each other:

My command is this: Love each other as I have loved you. Greater love has no one than this, that he lay down his life for his friends. You are My friends if you do what I command (John 15:12-14).

Jesus' love for us, which He proved by laying down His life for us, makes it possible for us to love Him in return. Sometimes that is the easy part. His love for us also makes it possible for us to love others. That's not always so easy, but it's where the rubber meets the road. Remember what John said in his first Epistle about those who say they love God yet hate their brothers—they are liars and the truth is not in them. No matter how much we might like it to be otherwise, if we are not right with our brother then we are not right with God. In fact, we cannot be right with God until we have resolved the problem with our brother.

Whatever Jesus expects of us or commands of us, He enables us to do. Our part is to respond in faith and obedience. Many times "the other guy" is not very lovable, but then a lot of times neither are we. Yet, the Lord dwells in him as much as He does in you and me. Remember also that Jesus taught us that whatever we do to the "least of these" brothers and sisters in Christ, we do to Him because He lives in all of us (see Mt. 25:40). However we treat them, we treat Him.

Actually, living out the Christian gospel is quite simple. You don't need a fancy theory or complicated plan book. Simply love the person next to you, or down the street, or across town; whoever you meet. Just treat that person next to you as you would treat Jesus and as you would like to be treated. Remember Jesus' command, "Do to others as you would have them do to you" (Lk. 6:31).

Jesus summed it all up neatly when a teacher of the law questioned Him regarding the greatest commandment. Jesus replied, " 'Love the Lord your God with all your heart and with all your soul and with all your mind.' This is the first and greatest commandment. And the second is like it: 'Love your neighbor as yourself.' All the Law and the Prophets hang on these two commandments" (Mt. 22:37-40). In other words, as Paul says, "Love is the fulfillment of the law" (Rom. 13:10b).

Jesus said that there is no greater love than that which would lead a person to lay down his life for his friends. Jesus did that for us and He expects us to do the same. Christian living means dying to ourselves, living for Christ, and, through Him, for others. We are not our own because Christ bought us with the price of His own blood. Our only life is in Him. Paul wrote to the Galatians, "I have been crucified with Christ and I no longer live, but Christ lives in me. The life I live in the body, I live by faith in the Son of God, who loved me and gave Himself for me" (Gal. 2:20).

Do you hear that? What is true for Paul is true for you. You were crucified with Christ. It is no longer you who lives, but Christ in you. *Christ is in you!* Not some blessing from Christ, but Christ Himself is in you.

This is why Paul also says, "The secret is this: Christ in you, the hope of glory" (see Col. 1:27). This is the key to the Christian life. You cannot live that life, but Christ can live His life in you and through you by His Holy Spirit. Everywhere you go you take His Presence so that others may encounter the Presence of Christ in you—in your love, mercy, graciousness; in the way you serve and bless and give; in the way you encourage and build others up. They see that other people matter to you. You place their welfare above your own, seek their good before your own, serve them without expecting to be served in return. That is true discipleship. That is living out your faith, not just talking about it. That is Christ-like living.

Jesus says that we are His friends if we do what He commands. What does it mean to be a friend of Jesus? It means living with Him in a relationship of love and obedience. It means remaining in the truth. It means walking in the glorious liberty of the sons of God. It means laying down our lives in surrender to His will and in sacrificial service to others. It means doing the things He did and living the way He lived. It means becoming like Him.

Chosen as Branches

Jesus said, "You did not choose Me, but I chose you and appointed you to go and bear fruit—fruit that will last. Then the Father will give you whatever you ask in My name" (Jn. 15:16). We did not choose to be branches. The Vine chose us to live in Him! God chose us to be His children before the foundation of the world. True, we each made a personal choice to receive Christ and become believers, but that was only after

His Spirit drew us. He chose us before we chose Him. Other-wise, we never would have chosen Him.

Since Jesus chose us, He has the right to put us wherever He wants to. It is not up to us to decide where we will be on the vine. That is His choice. *If we are living and walking in the truth, our lives are not our own. We are completely at His disposal.* Our part is to humbly seek to know His will and ask Him to reveal the places and areas of service and ministry where He wants us to be. When we abide in the truth and allow the truth to abide in us, then God will give us whatever we ask for in His name. If we put Him first, He will take care of all our needs.

This is another way of expressing what Jesus said in the Sermon on the Mount: "But seek first His kingdom and His righteousness, and all these things will be given to you as well" (Mt. 6:33). If we live for others, blessing them and serving them, God will give us whatever we ask in prayer.

John 15:16 also says that Jesus has appointed us to bear lasting fruit. This means that, like our position on the vine, the fruit we bear is not ours to choose. The fruit is not for us any-way. Have you ever known of a branch eating its own fruit? Of course not. The fruit is not for the branches; it is for the vine-dresser, the owner of the vineyard. The fruit we bear is for our Father and He chooses what will be done with it.

The only trouble is that the Father doesn't come and pick the fruit Himself. He sends others into the vineyard to taste and pick the fruit we bear because of the work of the Spirit in our lives. That's fine as long as we like the people He sends. Unfortunately, that's not always the case, and then we want to complain. *Lord, I've gone to all this trouble to bear this fruit and look what You're doing with it! I don't even like that person who is here to pick this fruit of love and life.* That is total-ly irrelevant to God because the fruit isn't ours anyway.

Neither is it for us. It is for whoever He decides it is for. He has the right to send anyone He wants.

Sometimes we wish we were somewhere else, in a different place or a different church or a different ministry, or that we had a different gift. If we are living and walking in the truth, our lives are not our own. They belong to God and He plants us where He wants us and expects us to bear fruit where we are. Someone might say, "Lord, I'm waiting for my ministry." You'll wait a long time if you don't get on with what He gives you to do now because if you don't prove faithful in little things, He won't put you in charge of much.

Think of wherever you are right now as a proving ground. God is preparing you for greater usefulness. It may not always be bigger or more important in the way that man measures such things, but what counts is God's measure. If we are faithful in giving ourselves to Him we will receive the reward that Jesus promised when He said:

Give, and it will be given to you. A good measure, pressed down, shaken together and running over, will be poured into your lap. For with the measure you use, it will be measured to you (Luke 6:38).

We want to glorify God in our lives if we truly love Him. Jesus said that we do this by bearing much fruit. We want to encounter the glory of His Presence, and He wants to see that glory reflected in us by the way we live and the fruit we bear.

Chapter Ten

Practicing the Presence

Following the truth does not come without cost. We have already seen how our "jars of clay" must be broken in order for the treasure of the glory of the Presence of God in our lives to be poured out upon others. If we are going to follow Jesus, we will have to pay a price. Every person who encountered Jesus was presented with a choice: believe or not believe, follow or not follow. The same is true today. Anyone who meets Jesus faces the same choice. Matthew records several important examples of people facing this kind of decision. Perhaps the most familiar one is the "rich young ruler":

> *Now a man came up to Jesus and asked, "Teacher, what good thing must I do to get eternal life?" "Why do you ask Me about what is good?" Jesus replied. "There is only One who is good. If you want to enter life, obey the commandments." "Which ones?" the man inquired. Jesus replied, " 'Do not murder, do not commit adultery, do not steal, do not give false testimony, honor your father and mother,' and 'love your neighbor as yourself.' " "All these I have kept," the young man said.*

> *"What do I still lack?" Jesus answered, "If you want to be perfect, go, sell your possessions and give to the poor, and you will have treasure in heaven. Then come, follow Me." When the young man heard this, he went away sad, because he had great wealth* (Matthew 19:16-22).

This young man thought he wanted eternal life until he learned the cost. Notice that his question mentioned nothing about *following* Jesus. He asked what he could *do* to get eternal life. He probably had in mind some further ritual he could perform or an additional law he could obey; something he could do within the comfort and convenience of his wealthy lifestyle. When he discovered that what he sought required following Jesus in a life of complete self-sacrifice, it was more than he was willing to pay.

Matthew records another occasion where people were faced with choices concerning Jesus:

> *Then a teacher of the law came to Him and said, "Teacher, I will follow You wherever You go." Jesus replied, "Foxes have holes and birds of the air have nests, but the Son of Man has no place to lay His head." Another disciple said to Him, "Lord, first let me go and bury my father." But Jesus told him, "Follow Me, and let the dead bury their own dead"* (Matthew 8:19-22).

Jesus was never ambiguous about the costs of discipleship; neither did He ever lower the standards. He laid them out plainly, encouraged everyone to count the cost before deciding, then challenged whoever would to follow Him. Some came with excuses; others with conditional commitment: "I'll follow you when…" or "I'll follow you after…." *For Jesus, discipleship meant **total commitment***. He said, "If anyone would come after Me, he must deny himself and take up his cross daily and follow Me" (Lk. 9:23). In his parallel account of Matthew 8:19-22, Luke adds this caution from Jesus: "No one who puts his hand to the plow and looks back is fit for service in the kingdom of God" (Lk. 9:62).

You see, it is one thing to *believe* in Jesus; it is quite another to *follow* Him. Truth demands a response. Belief involving nothing more than intellectual acknowledgment is not discipleship; belief resulting in action *is*.

FOLLOWING THE TRUTH

It is wonderful to have an encounter with Jesus in which our needs are met, but we must remember that *the primary focus of His ministry was not to meet needs but to make disciples*. He established and commissioned His Church to do the same. "Go and make disciples of all nations" (Mt. 28:19a). Meeting needs is an important part of the ministry of making disciples, but should never take precedence over it. We are to preach the gospel, as well as hold healing crusades; we are to teach people to obey Christ, as well as demonstrate the signs and wonders that are to accompany our preaching.

Jesus said, "Follow Me, and let the dead bury their own dead." There is death in the world, but there is life in the truth. Jesus is the Truth and if we want life we must follow Him. Following Jesus means believing in Him and placing our trust in the things He has said. It means walking in His footsteps, seeking to do the very things that will please Him, believing that as we seek first His Kingdom and His righteousness, all we need will be given to us as well (see Mt. 6:33).

The first priority in our lives as disciples of Christ is the Kingdom of God. Our focus is to be squarely on Jesus. The writer of Hebrews said, "Let us fix our eyes on Jesus, the author and perfecter of our faith, who for the joy set before Him endured the cross, scorning its shame, and sat down at the right hand of the throne of God" (Heb. 12:2). The Scriptures also promise that signs and wonders will follow those who walk in and proclaim the truth (see Mk. 16:17-18). Jesus Himself is to be the *focus*. We are not seeking signs and wonders as ends in themselves. We are revealing Him, making disciples who will themselves follow Him. *We are those who look ahead, not backward; we look at Him, not ourselves; we focus our eyes on Jesus and follow Him, confident that He will work through us by His mighty power.*

When we put into practice the teachings of Jesus and apply them to our lives, we will find that the truth will overcome the facts not only in our own lives, but in the lives of other people all around us as well. That is how the gospel is to be spread: not just in words, but in words and deeds. Paul told the Corinthians, "For the kingdom of God is not a matter of talk but of power" (1 Cor. 4:20). We need the words of the Kingdom, the words of truth, but we also need faith in those words to release God's power. Seeing the life and the power that is promised in those words without following Jesus for their fulfillment will ultimately result in frustration and failure. A divine encounter will have little lasting results unless we live and walk in the good of what God does in such encounters.

PRACTICING THE TRUTH

Some people think that all we need to convince the world is more and greater miracles. They point to people with great healing ministries and say, "We need more people like that." Although it would be wonderful to have more people with healing ministries, that by itself will never win the world. We tend to forget that Jesus spoke a curse over the cities where most of His miracles were performed because they still did not believe. He said:

Woe to you, Korazin! Woe to you, Bethsaida! If the miracles that were performed in you had been performed in Tyre and Sidon, they would have repented long ago in sackcloth and ashes. But I tell you, it will be more bearable for Tyre and Sidon on the day of judgment than for you (Matthew 11:21-22).

Today, the locations of Korazin and Bethsaida are barren heaps of rubble on a hill overlooking Galilee. It is wishful fantasy to think that simply having more and greater miracles will bring faith to the nations. That will come *only* through proclaiming the gospel in the power of the Spirit. The nations of the earth must be confronted with the Truth: Jesus Christ who died for the sins of all men and rose again, guaranteeing eternal life to all who believe. Only by belief in that truth is there hope for the world. Of course, more miracles occur where belief in the truth is present, but it is *faith* in the truth, not the miracles, that matters. God wants us to trust Him to meet our needs. More than that, *He wants us to walk in the truth, believing and trusting Him, and to let Him work through us, expressing the fullness of His life through our lives.*

The kind of work Christ wants to do in and through us is the same work He did when He was on the earth. According to Matthew, "Jesus went through all the towns and villages, teaching in their synagogues, preaching the good news of the kingdom and healing every disease and sickness" (Mt. 9:35). That was Jesus' mission: teaching, preaching, healing. He taught the way of God by word and example, preached the good news of the Kingdom of God, and then healed "every disease and sickness" to confirm that what He taught and preached was indeed the truth of God. That is the correct emphasis. Healing is not the focus. It confirms the Word of God taught and preached in truth.

We are missing the whole point when we want to cut straight to the signs and wonders, but neglect the preaching of the Word. Sometimes people will say, "We don't need any preaching tonight; we have the power of the Holy Spirit here.

Let's let Him work." Yes, it may be true that God will work there, but there are also many people who need to hear the Word of Truth. We need to preach and teach the truth because God wants to build it into people's lives so that they live by it every day rather than simply wait for some special service or healing crusade. Discipleship involves building up ourselves and others in the truth so that we will be able to walk in the glorious liberty of the sons of God.

BELIEVING THE UNBELIEVABLE

Throughout the four Gospels, one particular phrase from the mouth of Jesus occurs in one form or another more than 75 times: "I tell you the truth." Depending on the translation, it may appear as "Truly I say to you," or "Verily I say unto you"; the meaning is the same regardless. Now if Jesus is the Truth and everything that He said is the truth, why does He use this phrase? Is it simply for emphasis? I believe it has greater significance than that.

If you look carefully at the occasions when it is used, you will see that this phrase usually precedes a statement that Jesus knows will be met with unbelief. It is as though He is saying, "I know you will find this hard to believe, but this is the truth." For example, Jesus said, "I tell you the truth, anyone who has faith in Me will do what I have been doing. He will do even greater things than these, because I am going to the Father" (Jn. 14:12). It is easy to see how such a statement would be hard to believe. In fact, it seems almost blasphemous to suggest that we could do greater things than Jesus, and yet that is precisely what He said. On another occasion Jesus said, "I tell you the truth, it is hard for a rich man to enter the kingdom of heaven. Again I tell you, it is easier for a camel to go through the eye of a needle than for a rich man to enter the kingdom of God" (Mt. 19:23-24). Such statements as these stretch our faith to its limits.

That brings up another point about Jesus' use of "I tell you the truth." Often, when we read the Scriptures, we will find that the words that follow "I tell you the truth" will expose unbelief in our own hearts. Jesus' words challenge us to acknowledge our unbelief and bring it to Him, allowing Him to bring our belief into line with His truth. Then we can speak the truth over the circumstances of our lives and be set free from the bondage brought on by our unbelief. By expressing faith in Jesus' words, we remove the doubt that His words could be true for us today.

Many of the things Jesus says about the life of faith and about discipleship are preceded with the phrase "I tell you the truth." For example, Jesus told His disciples, "I tell you the truth, if anyone says to this mountain, 'Go, throw yourself into the sea,' and does not doubt in his heart but believes that what he says will happen, it will be done for him. Therefore I tell you, whatever you ask for in prayer, believe that you have received it, and it will be yours" (Mk. 11:23-24). This is a challenge to our experience because there are many times when we think that we believe, but we don't receive what we ask for in prayer. So God must have a different understanding of faith than we do. If we are to become faithful and effective disciples, we need to let such words as these challenge us, not deter us. Remember, the truth sets us free. When Jesus speaks a word of truth into our lives, He isn't seeking to overwhelm us, but liberate us. *He wants to see faith growing in our lives along with greater release of the power of His Spirit. This is possible if we will simply dare to believe what He says to us.*

Another statement Jesus made regarding discipleship is this: "I tell you the truth, no servant is greater than his master, nor is a messenger greater than the one who sent him. Now that you know these things, you will be blessed if you do them" (Jn. 13:16-17). If we are followers of the Truth, then we strive to be like Him: He was a servant, so we need to be servants; He preached the gospel, so we need to preach the gospel; He cared for the sick and hurting, so we need to care for the sick and hurting. As servants of the Lord, we need to be submissive to Him. We must allow Him to be Lord of our lives. Jesus' words challenge our faith, but also command our obedience to bring our lives into line with His truth. *Any cost God asks us to pay in order to follow the truth is far outweighed by the rewards that come for our obedience.* This is His promise:

"I tell you the truth," Jesus replied, "no one who has left home or brothers or sisters or mother or father or children or fields for Me and the gospel will fail to receive a hundred times as much in this present age (homes, brothers, sisters, mothers, children and fields— and with them, persecutions) and in the age to come, eternal life. But many who are first will be last, and the last first" (Mark 10:29-31).

One thing is certain. Whatever cost Jesus asks of you will not be too great for you. He always enables us to do anything He asks of us. He knows and understands our various capabilities.

However, He does take the faith factor into account. He often wants us to do what can be accomplished only through faith in Him. What He said to Paul is also His word to us: "My grace is sufficient for you, for My power is made perfect in weakness" (2 Cor. 12:9a).

THE HEART OF CHRIST

Becoming disciples of Christ means modeling our lives after His, seeking to make His thoughts our thoughts and His ways our ways. Paul says in First Corinthians 2:16 that we have the *mind* of Christ. However, we also have human minds. These we are seeking to bring into line with His mind, denying those thoughts that oppose the truth and hinder our encounter with Him. We need also to seek to know the *heart* of Christ.

This we can do by paying attention to both Jesus' words and actions. Matthew wrote, "When [Jesus] saw the crowds, He had compassion on them, because they were harassed and helpless, like sheep without a shepherd" (Mt. 9:36). The heart of Jesus is a heart of compassion. He Himself said, "Come to Me, all you who are weary and burdened, and I will give you rest. Take My yoke upon you and learn from Me, for I am gentle and humble in heart, and you will find rest for your souls. For My yoke is easy and My burden is light" (Mt. 11:28-30). Jesus had a gentle, humble, compassionate heart, full of mercy. Those qualities will characterize our hearts increasingly as we seek to become more and more like Jesus.

From His heart of compassion, Jesus saw that the crowds were like sheep without a shepherd. How did He respond? Did He simply meet their needs? No. He did much more than that. Certainly He looked upon their sick, took compassion, and healed them. Certainly He recognized their hunger and satisfied it, on one occasion feeding a multitude with nothing but the gift of one small boy's lunch of five bread loaves and two fish. As wonderful as these things were, they were not central. Jesus taught the people the truth, because in knowing the truth there was freedom.

Out of compassion Jesus forgave the woman brought before Him guilty of adultery (see Jn. 8:3-11). Hers was an open-and-shut case of sin, yet Jesus did not condemn her. He saw right through the scheme of her accusers, who cared nothing for her or her sin, but sought to trap Jesus. Nevertheless, they were ready to stone her until Jesus said to them, "If any one of you is without sin, let him be the first to throw a stone at her" (Jn. 8:7b). One by one all her accusers, under conviction for their own sins, went away until only the woman and Jesus were left. The one caught in sin faced the One who was without sin, and found grace. None of her accusers were left to condemn her, and Jesus did not condemn her either. He told her instead to "Go now and leave your life of sin" (Jn. 8:11c).

People often condemn others when they are not guilty of the same sin. This is a form of self-righteousness. Jesus did not say, "Let him who is without adultery cast the first stone," but "Let him who is without sin."

The fact that we sin at all means that we have no right to judge anyone. *All* judgment has been given to the Son! So none is left for us to exercise!

Paradoxically, when we are guilty of sin we do not want others to judge us. We beg for patience, tolerance, understanding, and mercy. Well, we are to do to others what we want them to do to us.

When we cultivate Christ's heart of compassion within ourselves, our primary concern will be not for ourselves and our needs, but for others. Our desire will be to be God's instruments and the channels of His life and grace to other people.

Another characteristic of the heart of Christ is a giving spirit. The clearest example of this is when Jesus gave Himself willingly for us on the cross. His death also reflected the Father's heart toward us. It is impossible to outgive God. Whatever we give to Him freely and out of love, He will give back far more. Jesus said, "Give, and it will be given to you. A good measure, pressed down, shaken together and running over, will be poured into your lap. For with the measure you use, it will be measured to you" (Lk. 6:38). This is true in every aspect of life, financial or otherwise.

John tells us in his first Epistle that we cannot live for God without living for others. If we want to live for the truth, we have to make the truth known to others. That means that all of us are witnesses to the truth. We believe it, speak it, and share it whenever and wherever there is opportunity. In this way the truth will impact the people whom we touch and change their circumstances. Paul told Philemon, "I pray that you may be active in sharing your faith, so that you will have a full under-standing of every good thing we have in Christ" (verse 6).

WORKERS FOR THE HARVEST

Another characteristic of disciples of Christ is sensitivity to the need for a spiritual harvest. Jesus told His disciples, "The harvest is plentiful but the workers are few. Ask the Lord of the harvest, therefore, to send out workers into His harvest field" (Mt. 9:37b-38). Millions of people around the world are lost, dying without Christ. Why then are there so few workers for the harvest? Could it be because so few really believe the truth and put their hearts and confidence in it? Are there too many Christians who are too in love with their comfortable situa-tions and easy living to go out and labor in the fields?

Jesus said that we should pray for the Lord of the harvest to send forth workers into His harvest. Where is the harvest? It is all around us. The fields are white and ready for reaping. We are surrounded by people who need to hear the truth. It is not enough to pray that more people will come in to our churches and listen to the truth. The Church has been trapped in that rut far too long. The world will not come to us. If we are to reach the world for Christ, we must go to the world where He sends us. That's why God is in the process of changing the whole concept and perception of His Church with regard to the har-vest. He is reminding us that *we are a people called to take the truth to the world; to carry to the nations the message of the divine life that is released by faith in the Lord of Truth.*

The heart of Christ reaches out to every person who is gripped in the darkness of the deception with which the god of this age has blinded the minds of unbelievers. God is raising up a people who will take the light of His truth where at pres-ent there is only darkness: to the rich and the poor, the desper-ate and needy, the blind and indifferent. Many of these people are quite content to live by the facts and to try to improve their lives themselves. In fact, they know of no other way. Whatever their circumstances, their need is the same: salvation by grace, forgiveness of sin, and impartation of God's life and power. They will not hear unless we tell them. That is why Jesus said:

> *You are the light of the world. A city on a hill cannot be hidden. Neither do people light a lamp and put it under a bowl. Instead they put it on its stand, and it gives light to everyone in the house. In the same way, let your light shine before men, that they may see your good deeds and praise your Father in heaven* (Matthew 5:14-16).

All over the world, God is giving wonderful promises of a coming time of harvest. It is God alone who gives the growth. Paul said, "I planted the seed, Apollos watered it, but God made it grow" (1 Cor. 3:6).

Because this is the case, we need to ask ourselves where God will give the growth. Obviously He will not give growth to a situation with which He is not happy, as in a church torn by division, or full of apathy and complacency, or where the people are full of judgment, or are just plain disobedient.

When will He bring the harvest? When His people are preparing their hearts and lives. When there is concern to reach out to the lost with the love and compassion of Jesus. Where His people have the ability, not just to welcome converts, but to make disciples.

The Lord has told us that if we believe, He will send a harvest. Then we had better get ready for it—both personally and corporately.

APPLYING THE TRUTH

The day came for Jesus' disciples when it was time to begin applying what they were learning. Matthew tells us that Jesus "called His twelve disciples to Him and gave them authority to drive out evil spirits and to heal every disease and sickness" (Mt. 10:1). Where did Jesus get His authority? It came from His Father. As Jesus submitted to the authority of His Father and walked constantly in the truth, He was able to exercise authority over physical circumstances. In like manner, our submission to Jesus—our walking in the truth, believing and applying it—gives us the authority to speak the truth over the circumstances of our lives and those of others to whom He sends us.

Jesus gave His disciples authority to do anything they had seen Him doing. In whatever way they had seen authority working in Him, that same authority had been given to them: healing the sick, proclaiming forgiveness of sins, binding and loosing. Their focus, however, was on the Kingdom of Heaven. Jesus told them, "As you go, preach this message: 'The kingdom of heaven is near.' Heal the sick, raise the dead, cleanse those who have leprosy, drive out demons. Freely you have received, freely give" (Mt. 10:7-8). Do you see the order of priority here? Preach the message of the Kingdom, and the miraculous signs will follow as confirmation of the truth of the message preached. Do we not long today for a Church that manifests such authority as this?

Why were the disciples to place such an emphasis on the Kingdom of Heaven? The Kingdom is the sovereign rule and reign of God. It is not enough for us simply to say that we love Jesus; we are to live as children of His Kingdom. We have somehow become extremely self-centered in just wanting a nice cozy love relationship with Jesus instead of really seeking first His Kingdom and His righteousness and seeing the authority, the life, and the power of God radiating out through our lives. Jesus said, "Freely you have received, freely give." *The disciples received the gift of the Kingdom; they were to give the life of the Kingdom. They had received the truth; they were to impart the truth. They had received faith in Jesus as the Truth to overcome; they were to share the faith that trusts Jesus to overcome in any and every situation. They had received the gift of eternal life; they were to give the gospel of the Kingdom of God so that same eternal life could be imparted to others.*

What a wonderful privilege God gives to those who believe in Him! How sad it is that so many Christians see themselves merely as survivors, rather than as channels of God's grace. Week after week they attend worship and other meetings hoping only to receive enough ministry to survive another week and get through life's problems. The world is crying out in desperation, longing for the sons of God—us—to be revealed; crying out for the truth. Before that can happen, though, we must understand that *we are to be mighty men and women of faith whom God is placing at the very heart of the revival that He is bringing to the nations.*

There is no answer for our world other than Jesus Christ, and His plan has always been to use us to take His message of reconciliation to the world. It isn't a question simply of having our doctrine right, attending teaching, and dotting every "i" and crossing every "t." Training and knowledge are important and useful, but God is able to use a believer from the moment of his conversion to impact the lives of other people with the truth. Sometimes the greatest evangelists are those who have just been saved themselves; the greatest preachers of healing, those who have just been healed. They are the witnesses because they have something to say. They have something to say not only because they believe the words in the Bible, but also because they have seen those words work in their lives.

This is why testimony is so important. As disciples of Christ, we have seen the power and the life of God working in our lives, and our witness to that truth can impact the lives of others. Faithful testimony gives all glory to God; it does not draw attention to either itself or the one testifying. We have a wonderful story to tell: that Jesus came to save us and that He performed many amazing signs and wonders. What is more wonderful still is that He has given that same authority to us so that we can continue His ministry and mission to the world.

We want to glorify God in our lives if we truly love Him. Jesus said that we do this by bearing much fruit. We want to encounter the glory of His Presence, and He wants to see that glory reflected in us by the way we live and the fruit we bear.

Chapter Eleven

Our Journey With Truth

God has given us a full and complete revelation of the truth. The Bible is the very Word of God, complete and self-sufficient. In it God has revealed all the truth we need to become believers and to follow Christ as faithful disciples. Concerning God's Word, Paul wrote to Timothy:

All Scripture is God-breathed and is useful for teaching, rebuking, correcting and training in righteousness, so that the man of God may be thoroughly equipped for every good work (2 Timothy 3:16-17).

The Bible reveals the nature and purposes of God and His dealings with mankind and teaches us everything we need to be "thoroughly equipped" to walk in the truth as children of God. It was inspired (literally, "God-breathed") by God the Father; Jesus the Son is revealed in its pages; and its truths are interpreted to our understanding by the Holy Spirit. God is the source and end of all Truth, Jesus is the Word of Truth, and the Holy Spirit is the Spirit of Truth—and They are all in accord. *Everything the Spirit of Truth says is completely consistent with the Word of Truth, Jesus, who is the perfect expression of God.*

Walking in the truth requires that we be deeply rooted in the Word of God. It is not enough simply to say that we "believe." We must remain, or continue, in the Word. *Remember that the only truth we really believe is the truth we **do***. That's what Jesus meant when He said, "If you hold to My teaching, you are really My disciples. Then you will know the truth, and the truth will set you free" (Jn. 8:31-32). Freedom comes from holding onto the truth.

Because of the many pressures and forces opposing the truth, however, it is not always easy for people to hold fast. In His parable about the sower and the seed (see Mt. 13:3-9), Jesus tells of seed being sown on "rocky places" without much soil. Plants sprang up quickly because of the shallowness of the soil, but withered just as quickly under the hot sun because they had no root. Jesus later explained that the rocky soil represented those who start off in the truth with enthusiasm and joy but, because they are not rooted in the truth, quickly abandon it when difficulty or persecution come along.

There are pressures all around us to pull us away from the truth. That's why it is so important for us to be deeply rooted in the Word of God. We don't want to be rocky soil. We want to be good soil: those who hear the Word and understand it, producing a crop that yields 30, 60, even 100 times the amount sown (see Mt. 13:23). *Those who bear the fruit are those who walk in the truth, holding fast to the Word of God with an honest and good heart, never giving up even in the face of opposition or pressure.*

APPLYING THE TRUTH

Walking in the truth means learning how to apply the truth to our lives and living in it every day. It isn't always easy, but we have the Holy Spirit within us who enables us to do it. The more we do it the easier it becomes. The secret is to make it *a way of life*. We must know and apply the truth in every situation and circumstance of our lives. It is not enough simply to read God's Word; we must have it in our hearts, in our heads, and on our lips. The psalmist wrote:

How can a young man keep his way pure? By living according to Your word. ... I have hidden Your word in my heart that I might not sin against You. ... With my lips I recount all the laws that come from Your mouth. ... Your word is a lamp to my feet and a light for my path. ... May my lips overflow with praise, for You teach me Your decrees. May my tongue sing of Your word, for all Your commands are righteous (Psalm 119:9,11,13, 105,171-172).

The truth cannot affect our lives until we have it on our lips. What we speak is what we believe. The problem is sorting out the truth in the midst of the confusion of conflicting thoughts, ideas, and influences that bombard us from every direction. Some of it comes from the Lord, some from the enemy, some from other people, and some just from within ourselves. What you speak reveals which of these conflicting thoughts you believe.

Suppose someone says, "I'm sick." That reveals that he believes the symptoms and the fact of sickness. What is on his lips reflects what is in his heart. Jesus said, "For out of the overflow of the heart the mouth speaks" (Mt. 12:34b). He will be bound by and live under the sickness he has spoken over his life. On the other hand, if the truth is in his heart it will be on his lips, and he will speak healing rather than sickness: "By the stripes of Jesus I am healed." The truth in his heart will set him free as he claims his healing and looks for the evidence of it.

You also need to take the shield of faith and use it against the negatives that both the enemy and other people throw at you. Many sicknesses begin with a thought, for the enemy likes to create fear. He suggests, "You will have cancer." If you accept one negative, he will supply another and another. "There is a history of it in your family." "Do you feel that pain? That's the sign." "You are about the right age."

Do not receive any such thoughts. Cast them off immediately. "I reject that thought in the name of Jesus! I refuse to accept any sickness in my life. Jesus is my health and my salvation." Speak blessing over your life, not curses.

Others may say to you, "Be careful you don't catch it." To that you immediately reply (silently but firmly), "In the name of Jesus I will not catch that infection. That virus has no place in my life. I praise You, Jesus, that You are my life."

You see, if you are truly going to walk in the truth and live by faith you have to be vigilant all the time.

We need to be careful that we are not double-minded: speaking the truth one minute and speaking the facts the next; one moment talking healing and the next reciting our symptoms to anyone who will listen. If we are going to hold fast in the truth, then we must learn to speak it all the time. We live in a very negative world, so it is important that we train ourselves not to allow or speak negativity into our lives. Negativity opposes the truth.

Walking as Heirs of God

Walking in the truth also involves learning who we are and behaving accordingly. Consider Paul's words to the church in Rome:

For you did not receive a spirit that makes you a slave again to fear, but you received the Spirit of sonship. And by Him we cry, 'Abba, Father.' The Spirit Himself testifies with our spirit that we are God's children. Now if we are children, then we are heirs—heirs of God and co-heirs with Christ, if indeed we share in His suffer-ings in order that we may also share in His glory (Romans 8:15-17).

The same Spirit through whom we become children of God has set us free from fear. In its place He has given us a warm, intimate relationship with the Father and the assurance that we are His. Because we are God's children, we are also His heirs, which makes us co-heirs with Jesus who through His resur-rection has become "the firstborn among many brothers" (Rom. 8:29b). Think for a minute what that means. *As heirs of God and co-heirs with Christ, we will inherit whatever Christ inherits.* Jesus told His disciples, "All that belongs to the Father is Mine" (Jn. 16:15a), and "Do not be afraid, little flock, for your Father has been pleased to give you the king-dom" (Lk. 12:32).

God has chosen us to be His children. Why did He choose you? Why did He choose me? Well, He specializes in the weak and foolish! However, He does not leave us that way. He makes us strong in faith and imparts the wisdom of His Spirit to us.

In His sovereign will He has the right to choose anyone He wishes. If we continue in the truth, we will begin now to enter into our inheritance, and later into complete fullness when we go to glory. No matter who we are or when we join God's fam-ily, we each receive the same inheritance. That is the meaning behind Jesus' parable in Matthew 20:1-16 about the landowner who hired men to work in his vineyard. Those who were hired at the last hour received the same wages as those who worked all day.

Paul says that we are heirs of God and co-heirs with Christ *if we share in His sufferings.* What does that mean? We may think we must share in His crucifixion. Paul does speak in Galatians about being "crucified with Christ" (see Gal. 2:20), but that is not what he means here. Sharing in Jesus' sufferings means that we endure opposition to the truth the way He did. Make no mistake about it, walking in the truth will bring us into conflict with the enemies of the truth. This should not surprise us, nor should we fear it. Paul told Timothy that "everyone who wants to live a godly life in Christ Jesus will be persecuted" (2 Tim. 3:12). However, Jesus promised His overcoming Presence as we face tribulation in the world (see Jn. 16:33).

If we share in Jesus' sufferings, we will share in His glory also. Jesus' words from the Sermon on the Mount are encouraging:

> *Blessed are those who are persecuted because of righteousness, for theirs is the kingdom of heaven. Blessed are you when people insult you, persecute you and falsely say all kinds of evil against you because of Me. Rejoice and be glad, because great is your reward in heaven, for in the same way they persecuted the prophets who were before you* (Matthew 5:10-12).

We are to rejoice and be glad when we are persecuted, Jesus says. We are to consider such cost as a privilege. So some suffering lies between us and our eternal glory. Let's not walk around with long faces, though, saying we are going to suffer for the Lord. Remember that we put our lives under whatever we speak. Instead, let's say we are walking in the truth as children of the King. That will make a difference in both how we think of ourselves and how we think of our circumstances, including any opposition or suffering that come our way. We need to keep the big picture. Those who oppose the truth are the instruments of the enemy. They are the weeds among the wheat. As heirs of God and children of the truth, we have no reason to let anyone put anything on us that is not the truth. We can simply refuse it in the name of Jesus.

Speaking the Truth Over Death

Because Jesus is the Truth He knew how to walk and operate in the truth. Speaking only the words His Father gave Him to speak, Jesus always spoke according to the truth, never according to the facts. In chapter 11 of his Gospel, John records what is probably the most astounding demonstration Jesus ever gave of the power of speaking the truth to change the facts.

Jesus received word that His friend Lazarus was sick. Lazarus and his sisters Mary and Martha lived in Bethany in Judea. Jesus was on the other side of the Jordan River when He got the news. As soon as He heard about Lazarus, Jesus spoke the truth over the situation, saying, "This sickness will not end in death. No, it is for God's glory so that God's Son may be glorified through it" (Jn. 11:4). He doesn't mean that God is glorified in the sickness, but that He will be glorified in the raising of Lazarus from the dead.

Jesus could have responded differently. He could have said, "Oh, no! Lazarus is sick and may be dying. What are we going to do?" He could have focused on the fact of Lazarus' sickness, but He didn't. Instead, He spoke what was in His heart: faith that the sickness would not end in death because He was the Truth who could change the facts. He didn't allow the circumstances to overrule what was in His heart. He recognized in Lazarus' sickness the work of the enemy and rose up in faith, speaking the truth against it.

That should be our response as well, not only to deathly illness, but to any illness or situation where we are confronted with things contrary to God's best purposes for us. Since we speak according to what is in our hearts, we can speak either for evil or for good. We can speak the facts or we can speak the truth. We can condemn ourselves to sickness, to poverty, to failure, or to defeat simply by what we say. Now, Paul tells us that there is no condemnation for those who are in Christ Jesus (see Rom. 8:1) but satan, our accuser, tries to condemn us in our own hearts. He puts all sorts of negative thoughts and feelings of guilt in our minds in an attempt to get us to believe things that are contrary to the truth.

For that reason we must determine within our hearts not to listen to the enemy's lies or speak over our lives anything that contradicts the truth. If we are children of God who are walking in the truth, we should speak only the truth, affirming it loudly and confidently wherever we go and in any circumstance.

Throughout the story of the raising of Lazarus Jesus is shown speaking the truth over the situation:

- "Our friend Lazarus has fallen asleep; but I am going there to wake him up" (Jn. 11:11b). That's truth. Jesus knew Lazarus was dead. He also knew that Lazarus would not remain dead. That's why He had said that Lazarus' sickness would not end in death. Death was not the final word.

- "Your brother will rise again." … "I am the resurrection and the life. He who believes in Me will live, even though he dies; and whoever lives and believes in Me will never die. Do you believe this?" (Jn. 11:23,25-26) Jesus spoke these words to Martha, His dear friend and Lazarus' sister, who thought He was referring to the general resurrection at the end of the age.

- "Take away the stone"…"Did I not tell you that if you believed, you would see the glory of God?" (Jn. 11:39-40) The stone was moved not to let the bad smell out, but to let Lazarus out. There is absolutely no doubt in Jesus' mind. The raising of Lazarus is as certain as if it has already happened.

- "Lazarus, come out!"…"Take off the grave clothes and let him go" (Jn. 11:43b-44). The truth overcame even the fact of death because death is not the truth. It is only a fact and therefore temporary. Truth is eternal, however. Jesus said that everyone who believes in Him has eternal life. That is eternal truth.

SPEAKING THE TRUTH OVER OPPOSITION

Walking in the truth will lead us right into the middle of spiritual warfare. It is unavoidable. As truth increases, so does opposition to the truth. It is like a plane breaking the sound barrier. As the plane's speed increases, air pressure and resistance build up in front of it until finally, after quite a bit of shaking, there is a *boom* and the plane breaks through. There is tremendous spiritual warfare going on right now because God has done so many major things in the world in recent years and continues to do more and more. Consequently, opposition is intensifying. *The very fact that opposition to the truth is increasing is a sign that God is getting ready to do something mighty and wonderful.* Someday soon there is going to be an explosion of truth like the world has never seen before.

We can see this pattern of growing opposition to the spread of truth as far back as the earliest days of the Church (if not further). Remember what happened in Jerusalem on the Day of Pentecost. The believers gathered in the upper room were filled with the Holy Spirit, and He took them to the streets of the city where 3,000 people were converted in one day. There were signs and wonders and miracles of all kinds. It was great. The more the believers proclaimed the truth, however, the more the opposition grew.

In the fourth chapter of Acts, Luke tells of the arrest of Peter and John for preaching the gospel. Hauled before the chief priests and elders, they were questioned, charged not to preach Jesus, threatened, and then released. Peter and John immediately returned to the church and reported what had been said to them. The gospel was advancing, but the opposition was strong and growing stronger. The Jerusalem church's response is a model of how every church and every believer today should respond to opposition:

> *When they heard this, they raised their voices together in prayer to God. "Sovereign Lord," they said, "You made the heaven and the earth and the sea, and everything in them. You spoke by the Holy Spirit through the mouth of Your servant, our father David: 'Why do the nations rage and the peoples plot in vain? The kings of the earth take their stand and the rulers gather together against the Lord and against His Anointed One.' Indeed Herod and Pontius Pilate met together with the Gentiles and the people of Israel in this city to conspire against Your holy servant Jesus, whom You anointed. They did what Your power and will had decided beforehand should happen. Now, Lord, consider their threats and enable Your servants to speak Your word with great boldness. Stretch out Your hand to heal and perform miraculous signs and wonders through the name of Your holy servant Jesus." After they prayed, the place where they were meeting was shaken. And they were all filled with the Holy Spirit and spoke the word of God boldly* (Acts 4:24-31).

The church didn't fret or whine or ask why this was happening. They didn't mount a public relations campaign to bolster their popularity or to discredit their enemies. They didn't even ask God to remove or destroy the opposition. Instead, they spoke the truth, acknowledging God's sovereignty, power, and the fact that the opposition they faced was in keeping with that endured by Jesus. They asked for Him to continue doing all that He had been doing: signs, wonders, and miracles in Jesus' name. *Their chief desire was **not** to be spared opposition, but to have **boldness** in the face of it. God honored their prayer.*

What an example for us! Our desire should be for boldness in the face of opposition, not avoidance of it. We won't be put off or put down by lies, deception, or any activities of those who oppose the truth. When the Spirit comes upon us, we speak the Word of God. We speak the truth because He is the truth and we speak it with boldness.

Isn't it good to know that we have the truth living in us? The truth is far more powerful than the lies of the enemy, far more powerful than any facts, far more powerful than all the forces of empty religion. So we must constantly feed on the truth because we want to experience its power. That is why the Bible should be the most-read book in our homes. We should read it and study it diligently and regularly. Otherwise, we will not have a deposit of truth within us to stand when the opposition comes. We should be so full of the truth that as soon as a problem arises, we meet it with the truth just as Jesus did.

We want to encounter the Presence of Jesus in our everyday circumstances, in our ministry to each other, in facing need, sickness, and opposition. We want to experience Him in His glory, but we want also to see that glory working through us for His further glory.

Speaking the Truth Over Existing Problems

How do we overcome something we already have, such as a problem, a sickness, or a need of some kind? The first thing to do is to remember that the problem is only a fact, not the truth. Jesus is the Truth and the Truth can change the facts. The next thing is to lay hold of that truth and walk in it. That means speaking it over our lives not just once or twice, but over and over, especially whenever something rises up to challenge it. It means not entertaining any thoughts or ideas other than the truth.

If you are sick, pray for healing, thank God for hearing your prayer, then claim your healing, speaking the truth of it over your life as often as necessary. This is not a magic formula. It is claiming and speaking the truth and training the mind and thoughts to conform to the mind of Christ. Sooner or later the words will hit you in the heart, and you will realize that it really is the truth. When you realize that it really is the truth, you will realize too that you are healed.

Maybe you feel really lousy or things are not going well for you right now. What do you say when someone asks you how you are doing? Don't focus on the negative. Say something like, "By Jesus' stripes I am healed," or "I'm rejoicing." Paul tells us, "Rejoice in the Lord always. I will say it again: Rejoice!" (Phil. 4:4), and "Finally, brothers, whatever is true, whatever is noble, whatever is right, whatever is pure, whatever is lovely, whatever is admirable—if anything is excellent or praiseworthy—think about such things" (Phil. 4:8). There is no need to tell anyone about the other things. Those are things we sort out with Jesus. He knows about them, we know about them, and that is all that matters.

It is a vital key to give thanks in all circumstances, for often it seems that the Lord will not lift a finger to help us until we do give thanks, exalting Him over the circumstances. While we complain and resent the situation, we are exalting the problem above our faith in Jesus. Giving thanks recognizes that Jesus is on the throne. He is in control. Our confidence is in Him.

Sometimes it helps to share with other people and get their good advice, but what we really need is the Word. It never hurts to ask someone to pray with you; to agree with you before the Lord regarding your situation and His truth that can change it. Remember the Lord's promise, "Again, I tell you that if two of you on earth agree about anything you ask for, it will be done for you by My Father in heaven" (Mt. 18:19).

Sometimes we spend our time talking rather than believing. That can be dangerous because when we talk it is very easy to focus on the facts rather than on the truth. The more we talk about the facts, the more we believe the facts and the greater the hold they have upon us. We put our lives under the power of what we say. If we talk facts, we are under the power of facts; if we talk truth, we are under the power of truth. What we say is what we get.

We want to speak the truth: to speak faith, life, healing, and rejoicing. We want to praise God in all circumstances because that is His will for us in Christ Jesus. We want to speak the truth in faith, knowing that without faith it is impossible to please God (see Heb. 11:6). We don't deserve such goodness and favor from God, but isn't it wonderful that He doesn't give us what we *do* deserve! He is full of grace and truth and He pours it out on us without measure.

We can thank the Lord that we belong to the truth; that He called us out of darkness into His light. Jesus' blood paid the price for our salvation. We belong to Him. Paul told the Corinthians:

> *Do you not know that your body is a temple of the Holy Spirit, who is in you, whom you have received from God? You are not your own; you were bought at a price. Therefore honor God with your body* (1 Corinthians 6:19-20).

We honor God by walking in the truth. We give Him glory!

Chapter Twelve

The Presence Comes to Stay

A growing number of Christians today have a heart-longing and hunger for revival. Perhaps you are one of them. The trouble is that there are many different concepts of revival. Some believers think that as soon as they experience any move of God either in their own lives or in their church that they are in revival. Many others define revival in terms of experiences and manifestations of the Holy Spirit. However we look at it, once we say that we are in revival there is a temptation not to seek God for anything more.

Most Christians seem to think of revival as the ultimate experience, an end in itself. We soak it all in and sit back with contented smiles on our faces, feeling that, finally, we have arrived. The danger is that if we now stop seeking more of God and His truth and life in our experiences, then we will rapidly lose even that which we have already received. The so-called "revival" will fade until it is nothing more than a fond memory.

In times of genuine revival God's children walk in the truth, living it daily. There is a consistency in their lives as they come into line with the Word of Truth and with the heart and mind of Christ more wholeheartedly and fully than ever before. Consequently, they have a more powerful influence and effect than ever on both the local community and the world beyond. *True revival in the Church leads to spiritual awakening in the world as the Church manifests the nature and life of the Kingdom of God in the power of the Spirit. I believe that is what God desires for us.*

Over the last 30 years or so we have witnessed numerous movements of God in different parts of the world, prompting many to ask hopefully, "Has revival come?" Yet during the same period the world has continued its steep decline in spiritual, social, moral, and ethical standards. Many major problems have gotten worse, and a whole array of new ones have appeared. Surely if we as the people of God were truly having the great times of blessing that we claim, then we would be seeing worldwide results. By all appearances, however, most nations of the world are completely oblivious to the blessings of God occurring in the Church. Clearly, something is missing.

I believe a big part of the problem lies with a Church that has become too inward-looking, focusing selfishly on our own blessings, healings, and spiritual experiences rather than on God's call to be witnesses of His resurrection power in the world. If true revival is to come, we must become world-conscious rather than self-conscious and God-centered rather than self-centered.

A pastor friend of mine with a church of over 200,000 does not speak of being in revival. Still only five percent of his nation are living as disciples; so there is no place for complacency, even though he sees about 1,000 turning to Christ every week in the central congregation alone. They are reaching out to God for more!

There are four truths for the Church that I believe are absolutely essential for revival: restoration of faith, consistency of walk, adaptability to change, and being dynamic in witness. There are probably many more. This is not a comprehensive list, but a church in revival will certainly exhibit these qualities.

Revival Truth #1: Restoration of Faith

We will not see the revival we want or the spiritual awakening and harvest among the nations that God has promised until there is a restoration of faith in the Church. Now someone may say, "Wait a minute! What do you mean 'restoration of faith in the Church'? As the Church, we *are* the people of faith!" *Christians as a whole need to return to a confident, dynamic, living faith that believes that the Bible means what it says and that God really wants to reconcile the world to Himself through Christ and that He will do it through the Church.* Many Christians and churches live with very little expectation of God moving in a mighty way or doing any great works in them or in the world. They neither look for nor expect revival. Consequently, it is unlikely that they will experience it. Revival flourishes in an environment of faith. Remember that Jesus was unable to do any miracles in His hometown of Nazareth because of the unbelief of the people.

There is no substitute for faith. Churches often try to "stir up" revival through fancy programs or new methods, but without the dynamic of Spirit-inspired faith these efforts are futile. We need more than just faith, but it is the place to start. We cannot receive what God has promised without that dynamic of faith within the life of the church. That's why in recent decades God has raised up the faith movement as a prophetic word to the Church as a whole. We don't have to embrace the particular teachings or manner of the movement lock, stock, and barrel, but we do need to pay heed to what God is saying to us about the importance of a dynamic faith.

Faith alone will not produce the revival, but we will never see revival without it. What the world needs is not more testimonies of our experiences, but the clear message of the truth. That's why Jesus came: to reveal the truth. How can we turn the world back to the truth if we don't believe it ourselves? Only as we believe the truth will we be effective in enabling others to do so. For you see, faith is contagious; if you have it, others can catch it from you.

The tragedy is that so many Christians who want to teach the Word lack a certain quality of experiential faith that could make their teaching really come alive. They are content simply to teach rather than to hunger to be men and women of faith who see the hand of God move in their own lives and in the lives of those to whom they speak in His name. Certainly, we want anointed teachers, but we need teachers who also move in that dynamic of faith so that when they teach, the power of God is released into people's lives. *We have nothing to teach unless we experience ourselves the message we proclaim.*

We might hear someone whose preaching or teaching is doctrinally and biblically faultless and yet lacks life and fire. Someone else could present the same truths, but with a dynamic of faith that kindles faith in the hearts of those who hear. As a result the power of the Holy Spirit moves upon people and dynamic supernatural events take place. There is power in the truth, but we must believe for that power to be released. The Church must be characterized once again by dynamic, expectant faith if we hope to see revival come.

REVIVAL TRUTH #2: CONSISTENCY OF WALK

Jesus commissioned His followers to "go and make disciples of all nations, baptizing them in the name of the Father and of the Son and of the Holy Spirit, and teaching them to obey everything I have commanded you. And surely I am with you always, to the very end of the age" (Mt. 28:19-20). This charge, known as the Great Commission, is the mission statement of the Church. It is a mandate from the Lord. Yet many believers are not really concerned about going into all the world and making disciples. They are more interested in having God satisfy their personal needs and desires.

Revival will never come as long as we have such a selfish outlook. We need to change our thinking so that we look outward instead of inward; instead of being self-conscious, become God-conscious and therefore world-conscious. *As God-conscious, world-conscious Christians, we will have a longing and a desire to impact the world with the life and truth of the gospel of Jesus Christ.*

Over the years we have witnessed many different efforts to fulfill the Great Commission. Missionaries have served and continue to serve sacrificially in many parts of the world for the sake of the gospel. Evangelists have mounted mass evangelism crusades all over the world that have seen powerful works of God and produced millions of conversions. Yet these efforts, as admirable as they are, have not resulted in changed nations. Often these "crusade Christians" have not become disciples, nor have they been built into local congregations. This is where the full dynamic of the Kingdom of God on earth is to be expressed, so that every community has a living testimony of the Kingdom in its midst.

Our commission from the Lord is to make disciples of all nations. Disciples are those who follow Jesus and walk in the truth. A critical key to revival and to reaching the nations is for God's people to demonstrate a consistent walk in the truth; a daily denial of self that seeks intimacy with God and follows Him in love and obedience. Great crusades and times of miracles and other displays of divine power all have their part in the total purpose of God, but more important is the building up of the local church. A sanctified church walking in the truth is the true vehicle for God's revival power.

The key to reaching the world is not a few mighty individuals with great ministries, but the entire Body of Christ equipped as He wants us to be: a prophetic people exercising the life, power, and authority of God to bring about the transformation of the nations. If a few can produce such results, what could the many do?

Charles Finney, the great nineteenth-century revivalist, maintained that we can have revival any place at any time as long as we are willing to pay the cost. I believe there are many Christians who are not willing to pay the cost of bringing their lives in line with the truth. They are ready to follow the truth as long as it is easy, comfortable, and convenient. *God is looking for people who will be totally uncompromising in their faith, in their obedience, and in their discipleship.* Dare we become such a people? We are the only ones who prevent it. God certainly desires it. After all, He gave us His Word and His Spirit to enable us to become just such a people. The decision is ours.

I believe with all my heart that God is preparing for the mightiest move of His Spirit that the world has ever seen. Even now there are signs that some nations have begun to experience moves of God greater than those of former generations. These movements of God must become more than temporary outbreaks if we hope to see the great harvest that God is promising. That calls for committed discipleship among God's people: a consistent walk in the truth. The Church as a whole must lay aside division and backbiting, resentment, bitterness, jealousy, and anger within and between local bodies. Instead, we must put on love and practice wholehearted devotion to the truth in submission to Christ so that the rivers of living water can pour out of our lives and transform the world around us.

There can be no revival without this consistent walk in the truth, both in the lives of individual Christians and in the corporate life of the Church. This is why the message of the truth has such dynamic possibilities. If we are faithful and consistent in our walk in the truth, we will see the fruit that God has promised. That is the challenge before us today as believers: to dare to bring our lives into line with the truth and live it, to speak it, and to share it with others without compromise. It is nothing less than a call to radical discipleship that Jesus has extended to every believer.

Who will respond to the call? Who will take seriously the challenge to walk in the truth consistently in order to see the revival that God is promising? Certainly there is a sovereign aspect to every move of God—He moves whenever and wherever He desires—but why does He choose certain times and places as opposed to others? *Is it possible that He waits for a people who genuinely hunger and thirst for the truth and who will genuinely make themselves available to Him as ambassadors of the truth?*

Revival Truth #3: Adaptability to Change

The church in revival is not locked into a mind-set that insists on doing things the way they have always been done. In fact, a revived church looks for and expects God to do new things in new ways, knowing that even though the message of the gospel never changes, changing times call for new methods and approaches for proclaiming that message. The church in revival therefore is flexible and not afraid of change under the direction of the Spirit. One of Jesus' teachings recorded in Matthew addresses this issue:

> *No one sews a patch of unshrunk cloth on an old garment, for the patch will pull away from the garment, making the tear worse. Neither do men pour new wine into old wineskins. If they do, the skins will burst, the wine will run out and the wineskins will be ruined. No, they pour new wine into new wineskins, and both are preserved* (Matthew 9:16-17).

There are several different ways to interpret these verses as applying both to ourselves as individuals and to the corporate Church. For instance, in personal application the old garment represents our old life of sin and the flesh, and the unshrunk patch of new cloth represents the new life in the Spirit which we received at our conversion.

On the corporate level the old garment signifies the Old Covenant of the law, and the new cloth signifies the New Covenant of the Spirit written on our hearts. The metaphor of the wine and wineskins teaches the same thing: The old wineskins represent the Old Covenant and the old life, and the new wine and wineskins represent the New Covenant and the new life in Christ.

A third interpretation, equally as valid as the first two, is that the old garment and the old wineskins represent the *unrevived* Christian and *unawakened* Church; the new cloth and the new wine and wineskins are newly awakened believers and churches moving forward in faith as God does new and wonderful things in their midst.

Jesus' point is that the new is incompatible with the old and must replace it. *We cannot attach the new life of the Spirit to the old life of the flesh.* Our old, hard, fleshly lives cannot contain the sweet new wine of life in the Spirit. The old and the new cannot be reconciled. We must die to the life of the flesh in order to walk in the life of the Spirit or, in other words, deny ourselves, take up our crosses daily, and follow Jesus.

The undoing of many Christians is when they try to live with a mixture of the old and the new. It doesn't work. It is impossible to improve or reform the old life. That is why Jesus put it to death with Him on the cross and gave us a new one. We have a *totally new* life, not a recycled old one. Paul wrote to the Corinthians, "Therefore, if anyone is in Christ, he is a new creation; the old has gone, the new has come!" (2 Cor. 5:17) Don't try to attach the new life to your old life. The new life has to replace your old life. We are brand-new people in Christ.

In the same way it is useless to try to contain the new things of the truth that Jesus proclaimed—the "new wine"— within the old, hard, inflexible, and lifeless religious structures of the past. The prophet Isaiah recorded the words of the Lord: "Forget the former things; do not dwell on the past. See, I am doing a new thing! Now it springs up; do you not perceive it? I am making a way in the desert and streams in the wasteland" (Is. 43:18-19). The Church needs to wake up to the new things that God is doing. That is what happens during revival.

We see this time and again. Every genuine revival has given birth to new churches and breathed fresh life into many existing ones. The existing churches that thrive are the ones that are open to God doing new and different things as well as doing old things in new ways; in other words, churches that are adaptable to change. Unfortunately, in every period of revival there are also churches and individual believers who are not willing to change, whether through unbelief, fear, or simply outright disobedience.

God will not allow His life to be limited by inflexible structures and traditions or by the disobedience of men. During revival God often shakes up the old structures, and if they do not move or change, He raises up new ones. We are beginning to see some of that in the current move of God. I believe that in the days ahead God will thoroughly shake His Church, bypassing those who are not open to change and giving birth to new ones who will not limit Him or try to contain Him, but shine His life brightly before the world.

Leading such a church could be uncomfortable. Many pastors want to maintain order and dignity and to contain everything under their control. Such an attitude reflects small faith and is the enemy of revival. *God is too big and mighty and powerful to be contained by the methods and minds of men.*

Revival churches will allow Him to burst out in their midst even if it means moving in new directions that express more fully the truth, the life, and power of Jesus Christ among His people.

Every congregation has to face the fact that if their present way of church was right in God's eyes, they would already be experiencing revival and having a powerful impact on the community. The only church that does not need change is a perfect church!

Adaptability to change will not come without a price. Not everyone in the Body of Christ will welcome or embrace the new things that happen during revival. Jesus broke all conventions in His quest to reach people, which is why He ran into such opposition, even in the synagogue. The leaders were not accustomed to healings occurring in the middle of Sabbath services. They got nervous when dynamic displays of divine power were released into their nice, neat, orderly, and traditional religious rituals. They didn't appreciate someone challenging the way they thought and believed. They didn't like the truth invading their comfortable little world and upsetting the "facts."

The same is true with many today. Those individuals and churches who are committed to walking in the truth and living in revival must be willing to pay the price of criticism, misunderstanding, and opposition that will come from many, even from within the community of believers.

God is preparing for the mightiest move of His Spirit in history, and one result will be the birth of many mighty new churches with a dynamic never before seen. Some of them are beginning to rise up already in different nations around the world. These new churches will break with the traditional and the familiar and will be totally different in their concept. In many ways they won't look or act like any churches familiar from past generations. Their focus will not be on meetings as much as on ministry, and their activity and presence will be found more in the marketplace than in a church building. Many of them may not even own a church building. While that is inconceivable to some today, it may very well be the hallmark of the future for the Church. After all, God is not concerned about buildings but about new wineskins—a people possessing a dynamic of truth and the power of the Holy Spirit that will enable great new things to happen throughout the world. Of course, any church will need to meet together for worship and for self-identity as the Body of Christ; but won't it be wonderful if the numbers of people who want to meet together are too great to be contained in a building? Dare we believe for such days?

Revival Truth #4: Dynamic in Witness

The church in revival will be dynamic in its witness worldwide. Everything that God does from the moment of new birth through the fullness of revival is the work of His grace. Paul told the Colossians that, "...All over the world this gospel is bearing fruit and growing, just as it has been doing among you since the day you heard it and understood God's grace in all its truth" (Col. 1:6). By God's will and grace the word of truth will grow and increase.

We have seen that the Holy Spirit's purpose is to direct us to the words of truth, to remind us of everything that Jesus has said. Revival does not happen without the continuing activity of the Holy Spirit, but experiences of the Holy Spirit are not in and of themselves revival. Those experiences help make revival possible as God's people return to the truth and live in the power of that truth.

From the moment of that initial great outpouring of the Holy Spirit on Pentecost we see wonderful things developing in the life of the early Church. It is very interesting and significant to note how the Book of Acts describes the growth and development of the Church:

- "So the word of God spread. The number of disciples in Jerusalem increased rapidly, and a large number of priests became obedient to the faith" (Acts 6:7).

- "But the word of God continued to increase and spread" (Acts 12:24).

- "Many of those who believed now came and openly confessed their evil deeds. ... In this way the word of the Lord spread widely and grew in power" (Acts 19:18,20).

All of these verses emphasize the fact this *the Spirit enabled the **Word** to grow.* We need to understand this in the sense that the Word was becoming living and effective in more and more people. The number of converts was increasing and the Church was being established in more and more areas. The disciples certainly understood that this whole progressive move of God was focused upon the spreading of the Word. *The early Christians believed the Word of Truth, were established in the Word of Truth, and walked in the Word of Truth, experiencing great power and effectiveness in dynamic witness everywhere they went.*

Acts 19:20 is interesting in another way in that it says that the Word increased in *power*. How does the Word grow in power? As the Word spreads, and as people believe the Word, the power in the Word is released into their lives and circumstances. It seems that the more faith grows within the life of the Church, the more the power in the Word is experienced by the Church. This is by God's design, so we should not see a weakening of faith as the Church spreads, but an increase. Whenever we believe the Word, the life and power that are in the Word are released into our lives and circumstances.

So often when we concentrate upon the experience of the Holy Spirit we see powerful things happening at first, but then the power seems to diminish. If we remember that the Holy

D *Destiny Image*
New Releases

Other
Destiny Image titles
you will enjoy reading

THE GOD CHASERS
by Tommy Tenney.
Are you dissatisfied with "church"? Are you looking for more? Do you yearn to touch God? You may be a *God chaser*! The passion of Tommy Tenney, evangelist and third-generation Pentecostal minister, is to "catch" God and find himself in God's manifest presence. For too long God's children have been content with crumbs. The Father is looking for those who will seek His face. This book will enflame your own desire to seek God with your whole heart and being—and to find Him.
ISBN 0-7684-2016-4 $11.99p

THE LOST ART OF INTERCESSION
by Jim W. Goll.
The founder of Ministry to the Nations, Jim Goll has traveled the world in a teaching and prophetic ministry. All over the globe God is moving—He is responding to the prayers of His people. Here Jim Goll teaches the lessons learned by the Moravians during their 100-year prayer Watch. They sent up prayers; God sent down His power. Through Scripture, the Moravian example, and his own prayer life, Jim Goll proves that "what goes up must come down."
ISBN 1-56043-697-2 $10.99p

THE POWER OF BROKENNESS
by Don Nori.
Accepting Brokenness is a must for becoming a true vessel of the Lord, and is a stepping-stone to revival in our hearts, our homes, and our churches. Brokenness alone brings us to the wonderful revelation of how deep and great our Lord's mercy really is. Join this companion who leads us through the darkest of nights. Discover the *Power of Brokenness*.
ISBN 1-56043-178-4 $10.99p

SECRETS OF THE MOST HOLY PLACE
by Don Nori.
Here is a prophetic parable you will read again and again. The winds of God are blowing, drawing you to His Life within the Veil of the Most Holy Place. There you begin to see as you experience a depth of relationship your heart has yearned for. This book is a living, dynamic experience with God!
ISBN 1-56043-076-1 $10.99p

Available at your local Christian bookstore.

Internet: http://www.reapernet.com

Other
Destiny Image titles
you will enjoy reading

RELEASERS OF LIFE
by Mary Audrey Raycroft.
Inside you is a river that is waiting to be tapped—the river of the Holy Spirit and power! Let Mary Audrey Raycroft, a gifted exhorter and teacher and the Pastor of Equipping Ministries and Women in Ministry at the Toronto Airport Christian Fellowship, teach you how you can release the unique gifts and anointings that the Lord has placed within you. Discover how you can move and minister in God's freeing power and be a releaser of life!
ISBN 1-56043-198-9 $10.99p

THE COSTLY ANOINTING
by Lori Wilke.
In this book, teacher and prophetic songwriter Lori Wilke boldly reveals God's requirements for being entrusted with an awesome power and authority. She speaks directly from God's heart to your heart concerning the most costly anointing. This is a word that will change your life!
ISBN 1-56043-051-6 $10.99p

REQUIREMENTS FOR GREATNESS
by Lori Wilke.
Everyone longs for greatness, but do we know what God's requirements are? In this life-changing message, Lori Wilke shows how Jesus exemplified true greatness, and how we must take on His attributes of justice, mercy, and humility to attain that greatness in His Kingdom.
ISBN 1-56043-152-0 $10.99p

Available at your local Christian bookstore.

Internet: http://www.reapernet.com

Destiny Image
New Releases

CORPORATE ANOINTING
by Kelley Varner.
Just as a united front is more powerful in battle, so is the anointing when Christians come together in unity! In this classic book, senior pastor Kelley Varner of Praise Tabernacle in Richlands, North Carolina, presents a powerful teaching and revelation that will change your life! Learn how God longs to reveal the fullness of Christ in the fullness of His Body in power and glory.
ISBN 0-7684-2011-3 $10.99p

EXTRAORDINARY POWER
FOR ORDINARY CHRISTIANS
by Erik Tammaru.
Ordinary people don't think too much about extraordinary power. We think that this kind of power is for extraordinary people. We forget that it is this supernatural power that makes us all extraordinary! We are all special in His sight and we all have the hope of extraordinary living. His power can change ordinary lives into lives empowered by the Holy Spirit and directed by His personal love for us.
ISBN 1-56043-309-4 $10.99p

ENCOUNTERS WITH A SUPERNATURAL GOD
by Jim and Michal Ann Goll.
The Golls know that angels are real. They have firsthand experience with supernatural angelic encounters. In this book you'll read and learn about angels and supernatural manifestations of God's Presence—and the real encounters that both Jim and Michal Ann have had! As the founders of Ministry to the Nations and speakers and teachers, they share that God wants to be intimate friends with His people. Go on an adventure with the Golls and find out if God has a supernatural encounter for you!
ISBN 1-56043-199-7 $10.99p

Available at your local Christian bookstore.

Internet: http://www.reapernet.com

Prices subject to change without notice. 4:49